DATE DUE	
OCT 8 1990		
OCT 1 9 1990	SEP 2 0 1994	
NOV 1 1990	MAR 2 0 1996	
MAR 2 0 1991	APR 6 1996	
APR 1 9 1991	NOV 8 1996	
JUN 1 1 1991		
JUN 2 4 1991	DEC 7 199	
FEB 1 0 1992		
MAR 1 6 1992	FEB 2 8 2001	
OCT 1 6 1992	APR 1 6 2001	
NOV 8 199	April 30 2001	
DEC 6 199		

THE UNKNOWN WAR

Freedom House

Freedom House is an independent nonprofit organization that monitors human rights and political freedom around the world. Established in 1941, Freedom House believes that effective advocacy of civil rights at home and human rights abroad must be grounded in fundamental democratic values and principles.

In international affairs, Freedom House continues to focus attention on human rights violations by oppressive regimes, both of the left and the right. At home, we stress the need to guarantee all citizens not only equal rights under law, but equal opportunity for social and economic advancement.

Freedom House programs and activities include bimonthly and annual publications, conferences and lecture series, public advocacy, ongoing research of political and civil liberties around the globe, and selected, on-site monitoring to encourage fair elections.

Focus on Issues

General Editor: James Finn

This publication is one in a series of Focus on Issues. The separate publications in this series differ in the method of examination and breadth of the study, but each focuses on a single, significant political issue of our time. The series represents one aspect of the extensive program of Freedom House. The views expressed are those of the authors and not necessarily those of the Board of Freedom House.

About the Author

Bernard Nietschmann is professor of geography at the University of California, Berkeley, specializing in Central America. He began studying the Miskito nation twenty years ago, and then became an advisor to the Indian resistance organizations Misurasata, Misura, Kisan and he is now advisor to Yatama. He is writing one book on the global wars between states and nations and another on his participation in the Yapti Tasba-Nicaragua war.

THE UNKNOWN WAR

The Miskito Nation, Nicaragua, and the United States

Bernard Nietschmann

Focus on Issues, No. 8

FREEDOM HOUSE

First published 1989.

Cover design by Emerson Wajdowicz Studios, N.Y.C.

Photographs on cover and throughout the book by Bernard Nietschmann.

Library of Congress Cataloging-in-Publication Data

Nietschmann, Bernard.
     The Unknown War

     (Focus on issues ; no. 8)
       1. Mosquito Indians—Government relations.
2. Mosquito Indians—Wars. 3. Nicaragua—Politics
and government—1979-   4. Indians of Central
America—Nicaragua—Government relations. 5. Indians
of Central America—Nicaragua—Wars. I. Title.
II. Series: Focus on issues (Freedom House (U.S.)) ; 8.
F1529.M9N548   1989   972.85'004978   89-7831
ISBN 0-932088-41-4
ISBN 0-932088-42-2 (pbk.)

Distributed by arrangement with:

University Press of America, Inc.
4720 Boston Way
Lanham, MD 20706

3 Henrietta Street
London, WC2E 8LU England

Contents

Combination of political + geographical factors relating to the state.

Geopolitics
and the Miskito Nation

War.
1989 - 1996

THERE IS A country east of the mountains and west of the islands. This country is located between Nicaragua and Cuba. Its continental shelf is the biggest in Central America or the Caribbean and contains proven oil deposits and the largest shrimping and lobstering grounds. A major maritime shipping route cuts across its waters. Its coastline contains more fish-rich river mouths, estuaries and lagoons than any other place of comparable size in tropical America. Its territory is bigger than Belize but smaller than Costa Rica and contains more lumber trees and grazing lands than either. Its many rivers—one is the longest in Central America—can provide huge quantities of hydroelectric power. This country has been militarily invaded and occupied several times, but it has never been defeated. It is currently fighting a seven-year-long war against an outside invasion and occupation force.

This country has a pivotal strategic location and an important geopolitical role in the Nicaraguan conflict—Latin America's most significant war. Historically, this country has been in the thick of other regional and superpower disputes and it is likely to continue to be so in future Central American and Caribbean conflicts.

1

This country is not in any atlas and it is not on most maps.

The Miskito people and nation

The Miskito have emerged as the world's best known indigenous people because of their present military and political struggle against the Sandinista state. At the same time, the Miskito are little understood because almost all descriptions and explanations have had the external goals of making the Miskito fit into European concepts of history, geography, ideology and nationality.

The Miskito have long seen themselves and acted as a distinct sovereign people with their own territory, resources, identity, institutions, language, ideology, history, nationality and nation. Miskito identity and expression as a territorially based nation-people predates the nineteenth century states of Nicaragua and Honduras, seventeenth century British claims, and, according to Miskito history, sixteenth century Spanish claims.

Europeans and their descendants have tried for almost half a millennium to annex the Miskito Nation (*Miskito Masrika*). But the Miskito people have not relinquished their sovereignty or territory by defeat, treaty or vote. Instead they have consistently sought to defend their nation by political and military means to expel would-be occupation forces and to establish bilateral treaties to recognize Miskito control over Miskito territory.

The Miskito consider themselves to be a people with a common historical identity and territory. They reject assertions that they are a Nicaraguan "tribe," "minority" or "ethnic group." No people living in their own nation is an "ethnic group." Ethnic groups live in other people's nations or states. (Are the Palestinians an Israeli ethnic group?) The concept of an ethnic group is embedded in state hegemony. An ethnic group is a substate population that maintains its own cul-

2

tural identity but not its own sovereignty, self-government, territory and resource base. Thus Managua defines the Miskito as a Nicaraguan "ethnic group" in an effort to cover-up its invasion and occupation of the Miskito nation.*

Bilwi (Puerto Cabezas) is the capital of the Miskito nation. Numerous nearby communities make this one of the highest population density areas in Won Tasbaia ("Our Land," the Miskito term for their national territory). The Wangki (Río Coco) historically has been the major population concentration of Miskito communities. River transport, rich alluvial soils and high concentrations of aquatic and terrestrial resources supported 400 miles of communities from Kip Almuk (Old Cape) to Yakalpani, the last Miskito settlement on Central America's largest river. In 1981 and 1982 the Sandinistas (Sangni Nani, the "Green Ones") burned down the Wangki and the people were forced into UNHCR (United Nations High Commissioner for Refugees) refugee camps to the north and Sandinista "relocation" camps to the south (at one time thirteen camps, of which only two of the five Tasba Pri—"Free Land"—camps were known to the outside world).

Most Miskito people live near or alongside water to the extent that those from the coastal communities are referred to as *auhya uplika* (beach people) and those from the rivers are called *awala uplika* (river people). Concentrations of coastal communities are found in the Sandy Bay Tara area, from Wawa to Kuamwatla, and from Sandy Bay Sirpi to Set Net.

---

* A nation is a geographically bounded territory of a common people who have a common ancestry, history, society, institutions, ideology, language, territory and (often) religion. Today there are between 3000 to 5000 nations in the world. Most nations have persisted for hundreds of years.

A state is a centralized political system, recognized by other states, that uses a civilian and military bureaucracy to enforce one set of institutions, laws and sometimes language and religion within its claimed boundaries, regardless of the presence of preexisting nations. Today there are 168 states in the world. Most states are 200 years old or less. More than one-half of the world's states did not exist before World War II.

Besides the Wangki, the most important Miskito river communities are found along the Wawa, Prinsawala (Prinsapolka) and Awaltara (Río Grande) rivers.

The Miskito nation has a land area of some 37,000 km2, almost twice the size of Belize (*Map* 1, p. 5). Cabo Camarón marks the northern boundary, Pearl Lagoon the southern, Yakalpani on the Wangki is the easternmost point, and Kip (Cabo Gracias a Dios) is the westernmost terrestrial limit. The adjacent Caribbean continental shelf, waters, cays, reefs and marine resources are also part of the Miskito nation. The cays include the Set Net Cays, Kings Cay, Taiira Cays, and Miskito Ki ka Tara (Big Miskito Cay). Tropical forests are located in the western and southern parts of the Miskito nation and an extensive pine savanna covers much of the northeastern area. Riverine tropical forests edge the abundant rivers whose floodplain soils are seasonally enriched by alluvial deposits. The principal resources of the Miskito nation include mahogany, cedar and pine wood; shrimp, lobster, sea turtles and fish; moderate amounts of gold and other minerals; and offshore oil deposits.

Since a 1960 World Court case (from which the Miskito were excluded), Honduras formally has occupied the northern one-third of the Miskito nation, and Nicaragua has made claim to the rest ever since its 1894 invasion. To the west of the Miskito nation is the Sumo nation and to the south the Creole and Rama nations (*Map* 2, p. 7).

The Sumo, Rama and Creole nations

The Sumo nation is made up of one large mountainous territory bounded by Nicaragua, the Miskito nation and Honduras. About thirty-two principal communities and another thirty or so smaller settlements comprise the main population centers. Musawas is the capital. Many of the communities are located along the Waspuk, Umbra, Wangki, Amak, Bokay and other rivers. Tropical riverine forests and tropical mountain for-

4

Title Page

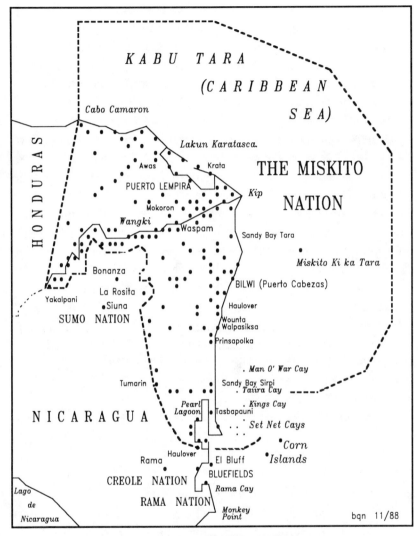

KABU TARA

(CARIBBEAN

SEA)

Cabo Camaron

Lakun Karatasca.

HONDURAS

Awas

Krata

PUERTO LEMPIRA

Kip

THE MISKITO

NATION

Mokoron

Wangki

Waspam

Sandy Bay Tara

Miskito Ki ka Tara

Bonanza

BILWI (Puerto Cabezas)

La Rosita

Yakalpani

Siuna

Haulover

SUMO NATION

Wounta
Walpasiksa

Prinsapolka

. Man O' War Cay

Tumarin

Sandy Bay Sirpi
. Taura Cay

. Kings Cay

Pearl
Lagoon

Tasbapauni

NICARAGUA

... Set Net Cays

Corn
Islands

Haulover

Rama

El Bluff

BLUEFIELDS

CREOLE NATION

Rama Cay

Lago
de
Nicaragua

RAMA NATION

Monkey
Point

bqn 11/88

MAP 1   THE MISKITO NATION

ests cover much of the Sumo nation. Mukuwas and other villages are in the gold-mining region but much of this area has been extensively deforested by Ladino migrants from the west. Outlier Sumo territories are centered on riverine forest areas in the lower Wawa River (for example, the community of Awastigni) and the middle reaches of the Banbana and Prinsawala rivers, on the edge of the pine savanna at Karawala near the mouth of the Awaltara (Río Grande), and in the tropical lowland forests—severely deforested by Ladino migrants—to the west of Bluefields and on several of the tributaries of the Río Escondido.

The main commercial resources of the Sumo nation are tropical woods such as mahogany, cedar and Santa María, and minerals, principally gold. During the Somoza dictatorships, American and Canadian companies operated gold mines in the Siuna-Bonanza-Rosita area. The Sandinista government nationalized the mines, but due to poor management, lack of repair parts and fuel, and frequent attacks by the FDN (Fuerza Democrática Nicaragüense, now known as the Resistencia Nicaragüense, or RN), gold production has declined greatly. One of the priorities of the Sumo people is to regain control over their nation's resource base, including tropical hardwoods, gold mines and mineral reserves in their territory. In June and July 1980 at Bosawas the Sumo organized one of the first demonstrations against the Frente Sandinista de Liberación Nacional (FSLN) to protest IRENA (Instituto Nicaragüense de Recursos Humanos y del Ambiente) attempts to cut down and take lumber trees off Sumo land. To demonstrate ownership, the Sumos built a wooden bridge on a road to IRENA's logging operation and began to charge a toll to the non-Sumo workers who came to cut Sumo trees. Defiant Sumos carrying machetes and axes blockaded roads to prevent entry to their land. The FSLN was forced to withdraw the IRENA loggers.

Although the Sumo are participants in the Miskito-dominated resistance organizations (Misurasata, Misura, Kisan, and now

6

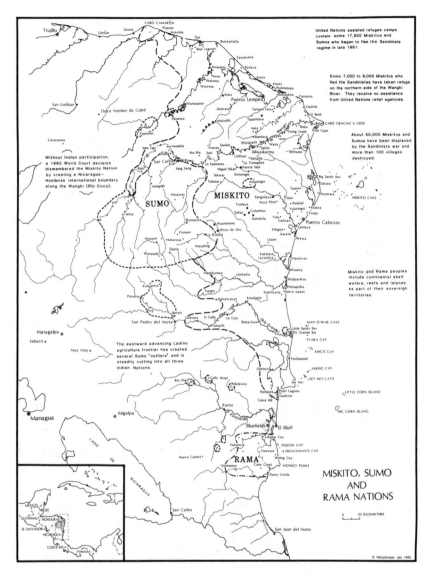

United Nations assisted refugee camps contain some 17,500 Miskitos and Sumos who began to flee the Sandinista regime in late 1981.

Some 7,000 to 9,000 Miskitos who fled the Sandinistas have taken refuge on the northern side of the Wangki River. They receive no assistance from United Nations relief agencies.

About 50,000 Miskitos and Sumos have been displaced by the Sandinista war and more than 100 villages destroyed.

Without Indian participation, a 1960 World Court decision dismembered the Miskito Nation by creating a Nicaragua–Honduras international boundary along the Wangki (Río Coco).

Miskito and Rama peoples include continental shelf waters, reefs and islands as part of their sovereign territories.

The eastward advancing Ladino agriculture frontier has created several Sumo "outliers" and is steadily cutting into all three Indian Nations.

SUMO

MISKITO

RAMA

MISKITO, SUMO
AND
RAMA NATIONS

0   20 KILOMETERS

B. Nietschmann July 1985

MAP 2 MISKITO, SUMO AND RAMA NATIONS

Yatama), Sumo leaders also have pursued independent means to defend their national territory and national interests. Sumo exiles have presented information in European capitals and at the United Nations in Geneva on Sandinista human rights violations and the destruction of over one-half of the Sumo communities. And in 1986 the Sumo opposition organization Sukawala presented to the Frente Sandinista a detailed plan and demands for territorial autonomy. To date, Sukawala has not received a response other than continuing occupation.

The Rama nation extends south from the Río Kukra area and mid-Bluefields Lagoon to the Río Punta Gorda and west along this river to its upper reaches. This area contains lowland and highland tropical forests, palm wetlands, part of a large coastal lagoon and offshore marine waters and islands (Frenchman's, Three Sisters and Pigeon Cays). The main Rama settlements are located on the lagoon island of Rama Cay, and at Wiring Cay, Cane Creek, Diamantes and Punta Gorda. The Ramas' natural resources are abundant fish, shrimp and oysters from Bluefields Lagoon, fairly good soils, and abundant tropical hardwoods. Control of the resource base is a main confrontational issue between the Ramas and the FSLN.

Early Rama resistance occurred when the Sandinistas imposed prohibitive price controls on all coast economic activities including oysters, charcoal and firewood, which were the Ramas' main source of cash used to supplement subsistence production. State expropriation of Rama lands and forests followed in 1980 and 1981, and by 1982 the Ramas were at war with the Sandinista occupation force. Although numerically small, the Rama fighters produced some of the fiercest fighting on the coast between 1982-1985. The Sandinistas bombed Rama civilians at Wiring Cay in May 1984 and at Rama Cay, July 1984. In April 1985, Rama comandantes "Coyote" and "Danto" led their men against the Sandinista EPS (Ejército Popular Sandinista) garrison in Bluefields with the intention of gaining desperately needed supplies. They al-

Miskito fighter inside Yapti Tasba.

most succeeded in taking Bluefields from the surprised Sandinistas. During the siege, the Creole MPS (Militias Populares Sandinistas) turned their weapons against the Sandinista army. The Rama attack against Bluefields and the Creole MPS uprising represent one of the major assaults against a Sandinista-held urban center.

Another indigenous people are the Creoles, whose distinct identity, history and territory evolved on the coast over several centuries. Their ancestors are mainly from Jamaica, the Cayman Islands and other Caribbean islands. Some married with Miskito women and lived in Miskito communities; their children grew up as Miskito. Others built or settled in new communities largely in the area between the Miskito and Rama nations. The principal Creole communities are Bluefields, The Bluff, Pearl Lagoon, Marshall Point, Brown Bank, and Corn Islands (Big and Small Corn Islands). Another part of the Creole nation is located along the coast south of the Rama nation including settlements at Corn River, Río Indio, Cocal and Greytown (San Juan del Norte). These were hard hit in the 1982-1986 fighting between the Sandinista EPS and Edén Pastora's ARDE (Alianza Revolucionaria Democrática).

Many Creole people depend on sea resources (shrimp, fish, lobster), small-scale agriculture, or wage-paying jobs for their livelihood. When the Cuban brigadistas came to Bluefields in 1980 to take control of and restructure the Creole work force, they were confronted with a massive October demonstration. The Creole people wanted to organize themselves with their own leaders. The Sandinistas sent in an 800-man elite unit to smash the demonstration, killed three people and wounded eleven, arrested many people, and forced the main leaders to flee to Costa Rica. (Two years later Edén Pastora went to Costa Rica to raise his ARDE guerrilla force but he failed to integrate the Creole exiles and refugees because it was Pastora who had led the Sandinista military assault against the civilian Creole demonstration in Bluefields.) Sandinista attempts to dominate Creole shrimp and lobster fishing largely have failed and INPESCA (Instituto Nicaragüense de La Pesca) has become one of the most despised occupation government organizations on the coast. A main objective of many Creole resistance leaders is to expel INPESCA and to exercise Creole management over Creole sea resources.

Before Hurricane "Joan," lobster fishing allowed Corn Island the most freedoms of any place under the Sandinista occupation. The FSLN desperately needs foreign earnings from lobster exports and to compete with Colombian buyers from San Andrés they must pay the Corn Island lobstermen U.S. $3.00 per pound for lobster tails. Nevertheless, approximately one-half of the catch is sold on the high seas to San Andrés and Limón buyers who use high-speed boats to bring frozen chicken, gasoline, motor oil, motor parts and clothes to sell to the Corn Islanders and buy lobster tails at $4.00 per pound. To encourage lobster fishing, the FSLN at first did not impose military conscription (Servico Militar Patriótico) in Corn Island, but this changed in 1987 and as a result scores of Corn Island youths have fled to the Cayman Islands, San Andrés and Costa Rica.

On 22 October 1988 Hurricane "Joan" hit Corn Island and Bluefields and destroyed 95 percent of the homes, buildings, trees, crops, wells and boats, and crippled the fishing industry. The hurricane also destroyed the communities of Rama Cay, Pearl Lagoon, Haulover, Raitipura, Kakabila, Kukra Hill and Rama, which is on the border between Nicaragua and Yapti Tasba.

Yapti tasba (motherland)

The Miskito, Sumo, Rama and Creole nations comprise "Yapti Tasba" (Motherland), the multinational East Coast territory whose autonomous status is the focus of the Indian war against the FSLN that began in 1981 and the negotiations that began

11

in 1984. The passage of colonial powers and central state governments is marked by the waste pile of cartographic terms that have been imposed on Yapti Tasba: La Costa Mosquitia, La Reserva Mosquitia, Departamento de Zelaya, La Mosquitia, Gracias a Dios, Costa Atlántica, Zelaya Norte, Zelaya Sur, Zona Especial I, Zona Especial II, La Región Autónoma Zelaya Norte, and La Región Autónoma Zelaya Sur.

The area of Yapti Tasba occupied by Nicaragua extends from Kip (Cabo Gracias a Dios) west along the Wangki (Río Coco) to Yakalpani, the last Miskito settlement located in what the Nicaraguans call Jinotega. From Yakalpani the Yapti Tasba boundary runs southeast to a hill called Sahsa (Saslaya II), thereby encompassing the Sumo nation, and then runs southward to San Pedro del Norte on the Awaltara (Río Grande) and then eastward along this river to the Miskito community of Tumarin (Tumarín in Spanish). From Tumarin, the boundary extends southerly to Rama on the Río Escondido territory and continues south to the headwaters of the Río Punta Gorda west of Atlanta. From there the boundary continues south to the confluence of the Río Sarapiquí and the Río San Juan. The Yapti Tasba boundary then extends eastward along the southern shore of Río San Juan to the sea. From the mouth of the Río San Juan, the sea boundary runs northeast along the edge of the continental shelf passing well to the east of Big and Little Corn Islands and Miskito Ki ka Tara (Big Miskito Cay), and then it extends west to Kip on the mainland (*Map* 3, p. 13). The land area of Yapti Tasba is 50,000 km2 and the sea area is 60,000 km2.

The Sandinistas do not want to accept the existence of the Miskito nation or of Yapti Tasba. But the first people to fight against them and the first to negotiate with them are from the Miskito nation. And those people want territorial autonomy, self-government and self-determination for the Miskito nation.

To control the Miskito people's demands for an end to

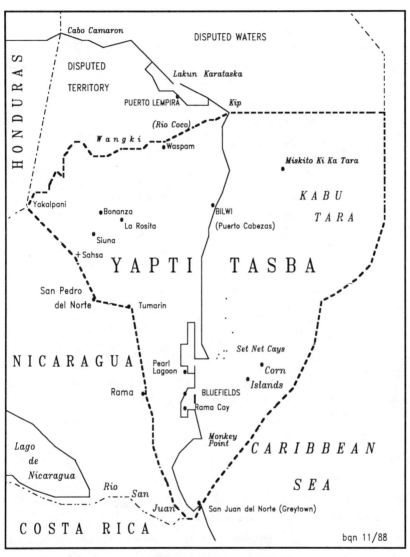

Cabo Camaron

DISPUTED WATERS

HONDURAS

DISPUTED
TERRITORY

Lakun Karataska

PUERTO LEMPIRA

Kip

(Rio Coco)

Wangki

●Waspam

Miskito Ki Ka Tara
●

●Yakalpani

●Bonanza
● *La Rosita*
●Siuna
+ Sahsa

/BILWI
(Puerto Cabezas)

KABU

TARA

Y A P T I   T A S B A

San Pedro
del Norte ●
● Tumarin

N I C A R A G U A

Pearl
Lagoon

..· *Set Net Cays*

● *Corn*
  Islands

Rama ●

BLUEFIELDS
●Rama Cay

Monkey
Point

Lago
de
Nicaragua

Rio
San
Juan

● San Juan del Norte (Greytown)

C A R I B B E A N

S E A

C O S T A   R I C A

bqn 11/88

MAP 3   YAPTI   TASBA

the occupation and for recognition of their historically autonomous territory, the FSLN imposed its own autonomy project in December 1984. After almost three years of "consultations" with the East Coast peoples, the FSLN's Autonomy Commission (no Indians allowed) and the Sandinista National Assembly drew up a Soviet-style autonomy statute which President Daniel Ortega signed on 7 September 1987, making it Nicaragua's official occupation policy. The FSLN's autonomy project is an attempt to shift control of Yapti Tasba from Sandinistas in Managua to Sandinistas in Puerto Cabezas and Bluefields. Another aim of the autonomy project is to turn around the Sandinistas' international image of aggression against Indian peoples.

puppet status Under the FSLN's Autonomy Statute, the northern and southern "autonomous governments" will have but puppet status under Frente Sandinista tutelage. When they are elected (elections have been postponed several times and as this is written are promised for May 1989), these "autonomous governments" will have only the power to "participate in the enactment" of FSLN programs and policies, to "administer" these programs and policies, and to "elaborate proposals" for legislation to regulate natural resource use and conservation (Article 8). FSLN autonomy does not permit self-determination, self-government, or resource control by the peoples of Yapti Tasba. To make sure, Article 24 states that "all resolutions and ordinances" of the autonomous governments have to be "in harmony" with the FSLN's constitution and laws. Furthermore, Nicaraguans who have been in Yapti Tasba for five or more years are deemed to be residents under the Autonomy Statute and are granted the right to vote, run for political office, and to lay claim to land and resources.

Sand. plan The FSLN drummed up an "autonomy law" that is nothing more than a plan for annexation by migration. The FSLN strategy is first to place the occupied territories under puppet rule backed by state security and military forces, then to muffle and eventually water down resistance by large-scale immigration of Party loyalists from the West Coast, and then to call for "democratic elections" when there is a comfortable majority of invaders in Yapti Tasba.

The territorial autonomy of Yapti Tasba has been a central issue in the first three rounds of the 1988 peace negotiations between Yatama (the United Nations of Yapti Tasba) and the Sandinistas. The 2 February 1988 "Preliminary Accords" signed between representatives of the two sides include recognition "of the right of the people of the Atlantic Coast to the lands and waters that they have occupied and worked traditionally which form an inalienable territory."

The location and size of this "inalienable territory" was a major dispute in the negotiations. During the March 1988 second round, the FSLN argued that the territory should be the same size as the Departamento de Zelaya in order for Managua to include another 100,000 Ladino people into the autonomous territory as a means to dilute Indian land rights. Yatama argued that Yapti Tasba was smaller than the Departamento de Zelaya and that the indigenous nations were seeking guaranteed rights over their own land, not Ladino land.

Yapti Tasba has a population of over 260,000, made up of four territorially-based original nations and Nicaraguan (Ladino) immigrants. Of the 70,000 Ladinos, some 20,000 are part of the FSLN occupation forces (military, security, political and settler).

Miskito nation	150,000
Rama nation	1,000
Ladinos	70,000
Sumo nation	13,000
Creole nation	30,000
	264,000

15

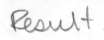

The Sandinista war in Yapti Tasba has destroyed one-half of the Miskito, Sumo and Rama communities and displaced more than one-half of the Indian and Creole peoples. The Miskito nation, for example, has suffered its own diaspora due to the Sandinista invasion and óccupation (erroneously called "counterinsurgency") that has burned villages and carried out forced relocations that have caused 50,000 people to flee as refugees and exiles to fourten different countries, from Canada to Peru.

Miskito sturka (Miskito history)

The past is not history. History is the reconstructed past that is important to a people. As a result there is one past and many histories. Two histories are in collision in the same area known by different names: Yapti Tasba and eastern Nicaragua-Honduras. One is a history of defense against invasion and the other is a history justifying attempts at occupation.

Miskito history of the Miskito nation traces the evolution of a common people that has developed along the eastern shoreline and lowland rivers of the Kabu Tara (the Caribbean). These people came to share a common sense of identity through language, and social, economic and political institutions that united individual communities within a communal territory. Centuries ago a powerful leader named Miskut organized the *Awala Uplika* (river people) and *Auhya Uplika* (beach people) into the Miskito masrika (Miskito nation) that then expanded westward up rivers and north and south along the coastline, absorbing into the Miskito nation those that did not flee or give tribute. Miskito history then resembles the history of most nations worldwide: unity, absorption, stability.

European history of the Miskito people begins, of course, with the Europeans and European explanations for what happened to them when they intruded into what was another people's country. This history is a history of attempted occupa-

16

tion which spans several centuries to the present and emphasizes the illegitimacy of Miskito nationhood in order to promote European claims to coveted territory and resources. As a result, this white history of a brown people purports that 1) the Miskito are a "recent" people who were "created" by colonialism (this is the *real* creation myth), 2) they are a "mixed" people due to assimilation of some Sumo and shipwrecked Black slaves (why is it that only Indian and not white blood mixes to create "unauthentic" peoples?), and 3) that the Miskito have a "retarded" history that has left them "politically backward" (this is racist Sandinista-speak that means the only good Indian is a Ladino).

Nineteenth-century United States writing on the Miskito nation tried to trivialize the existence of Miskito kings in an effort to portray them as an artificial prop to the British presence astride a potential inter-ocean canal route sought by the United States.[1] But the Miskito kings served for 250 years —longer than the United States has been independent from Britain—and they obviously must have had a "social base," to put it in today's terminology.[2]

In the mid-twentieth century the Miskito nation became a focus of anthropological study, typically the surest way to trivialize a people. But the Miskito endured the attempts to categorize them as "a tribe," "peasants," "a purchase society," and "a colonial creation."[3]

The FSLN has manufactured three recent histories of the Miskito people. The Sandinistas first justified their invasion by claiming they came to liberate the Miskito from a history of colonialist exploitation and persecution. When the Miskito rejected being forced into the Sandinista revolution as "New Indians" by being stripped of their land, government, leaders, resources, identity, society and economy, and took up arms to defend their nation, the Sandinistas conjured up another history for the Miskito. Instead of victims of colonialism, the Miskito were now said to be dupes of imperialism, meaning

17

This Miskito woman wears black to mourn her sixty-five-year-old husband, tortured to death by FSLN forces, October 1982.

that Indian peoples wouldn't defend their communities and territory unless put up to it by the CIA, Moravian and Catholic churches, and "somocista contras." Later, when the FSLN wanted to negotiate with Misurasata, the Sandinistas dumped the dupes of imperialism history and produced a third history. This is the Sandinista "error" history in which the so-called "errors" are never detailed and they always happened in the past.

In the white history, the Miskito are always the bystanders, never the protagonists, always the victims, never the victors. Miskito resistance to foreign intrusion and occupation extends over hundreds of years. When Europeans came, the Miskitos' collective response was straightforward: defend against those who tried military occupation and forced taxation, and trade with the rest. The Spaniards tried to invade, annex and tax, and were repulsed; the British entered to trade, and they stayed for more than 200 years. From the mid-1600s to late 1800s free trade and commerce propelled the Miskito nation economically into being the most prosperous region in Central America. This occurred due to abundant natural resources, the industriousness of the Miskito, the proximity to British maritime trade, and the absence of Spanish taxes that constrained the economic development of most of the rest of Central America. Spanish authorities ranted against Miskito free trade and the British presence.[4]

Centuries ago the superpowers were Britain and Spain, which, like today's superpowers, chose to fight their wars abroad in other peoples' countries and waters. A zone of British-Spanish conflict extended along the western Caribbean coastline from Belize to Cartagena. Within this area another long-term war raged between the Miskito and Spanish armies and navies.

Miskito sovereignty, trade and prosperity were threatened by Spanish colonialism and to keep their nation free, the Miskito fought successfully to hold back Spanish territorial advances. One author compiled but a partial listing of Miskito-

Spanish military battles that describes twenty-five between 1643 and 1814.[5] This does not include the 1711 naval incident on Lake Nicaragua when Spanish ships refused to engage Miskito craft, or the 1723 naval engagement when the Miskito "totally destroyed a Spanish expeditionary force off the Honduran coast."[6] In 1800 a Miskito army defeated and ousted the Spanish military garrison at Black River, putting an end to thirty years of Spanish occupation in the northern part of the Miskito nation. Thus the Miskito reasserted sovereignty over their entire nation twenty-one years before other anti-Spanish wars of independence led to the creation of Central American states.

The Miskito used diplomatic as well as military means to protect and reinforce their territorial sovereignty and to advance their national interests. "In 1711, and again in 1721, the Miskitos offered formal trade treaties with the governor of Costa Rica, who went so far as to receive and dine with the Miskito king in his palace, but would sign no treaty without Miskito submission to Spanish sovereignty."[7] No treaty was signed.

The nineteenth-century geopolitical struggle for possible inter-oceanic canal routes pitted the United States against Britain, and Britain was a trade ally of the Miskito nation. The most promising inter-oceanic route was the Río San Juan–Lake Nicaragua waterlink and the narrow Rivas Isthmus where a canal could be excavated to the Pacific. However, the British-Miskito domain over the proposed canal's Caribbean gateway blocked United States aspirations. Therefore, the United States used its pubescent power to 1) dislodge Britain and to deny the existence of Miskito territorial sovereignty and regional military-economic agreements that extended from Belize to Panama, and thus 2) replace the British-Miskito alliance with a United States-Nicaraguan alliance.

For the next sixty years foreign states made treaties between themselves over the Miskito nation without the consent or representation of the Miskito government. In 1850 the Clay-

20

ton-Bulwar treaty (U.S., Nicaragua and Great Britain) recognized less than one-half of the territory of the Miskito nation. As a result, Miskito leaders made several diplomatic missions to get these three governments to recognize their entire territory. United States Secretary of State, Mr. Marcy, wrote responses in 1853 and 1856 to the Miskito demand that their nation be recognized:

> They have only possessory rights to the country they occupy and not sovereignty of it.
>
> The President cannot admit as true, and therefore cannot under any possible circumstances advise the Republic of Nicaragua to admit that the Mosquito Indians are a State or Government any more than a band of Maroons in the island of Jamaica are a State or Government.

In the 1860 Treaty of Managua Great Britain gave to Nicaragua something it did not have—sovereignty over the Miskito nation (the Rama and Sumo nations were not mentioned):

> Article I. Her Britannic Majesty...will recognize as belonging to and under the sovereignty of the Republic of Nicaragua, the country hitherto occupied or claimed by the Mosquito Indians within the frontiers of the Republic, whatever that frontier may be.

The Miskito government was not a participant in the treaty nor did it agree to the treaty. The treaty attempted to reduce the area of the Miskito nation by two-thirds and to convert it into a "Mosquito Reserve."

> Article II. A district within the territory of the Republic Nicaragua shall be assigned to the Mosquito Indians, which district shall remain, as above stipulated, under the sovereignty of the Republic of Nicaragua....

At the same time, Miskito self-government was recognized and protected by the treaty and this was later upheld in an 1878 arbitration decision by Austria's Emperor Franz Joseph to whom Nicaragua and Britain turned to settle disputes over the treaty.[8]

Before they left in the late nineteenth century, the British did do land surveys throughout the Miskito nation and gave each community a map and title to its lands.

The Miskito nation regarded the 1860 Treaty of Managua as illegitimate. During the next thirty years, more and more British settlers and traders left and more and more American business interests arrived. Export of mahogany, cedar, pinewood and natural rubber accelerated—work was abundant and wages were good. The Miskito nation continued to prosper and Bluefields and Puerto Cabezas were among the most developed and thriving towns anywhere in Central America.

This prosperity and Nicaragua's own ocean-to-ocean geographic lust culminated in Nicaraguan President Zelaya ordering a military invasion of the Miskito nation, February 1894, on the ridiculous pretext of protecting it from a Honduran invasion (similar to the Sandinistas' 1981 invasion excuse of protecting the Miskito from the contras). Desperately short of weapons, people bravely fought Zelaya's army and succeeded in forcing it out of Bluefields for six months. The British were to supply 600 rifles to the Miskito, most likely transferred from the British naval ship Cleopatra anchored off Bluefields, but a U.S. Navy captain divulged the location of the arms cache to Zelaya's army, the arms were seized, and Bluefields was taken in August 1894.

Some eighty-eight years later the United States would reverse its support of Nicaragua and would give weapons to the Miskito. However, the small number and poor quality of the weapons led some Miskito combatants to ask if Washington was just then passing on the 1894 rifles! The one con-

22

stant in the Miskito people's political alliances with colonial and modern states is their need for equivalent weapons to defend their nation, territory and communities.

Nicaraguan President Zelaya—the father of his country to the Sandinistas—proceeded to organize in February 1895 a hangman's court that he called "The Mosquito Convention," to further impose the invasion that for 400 years had been and was continuing to be resisted. A handful of Miskitos were rounded up and they were coerced to sign a shotgun-marriage agreement for the "reincorporation" of the coast to Nicaragua (even the Chinese didn't call their 1950s invasion of Tibet a "reincorporation"!). Appropriately, President Zelaya named the occupied country, the "Departamento de Zelaya," invited in the United Fruit Company, and began to sack the Miskito nation. As the Sandinistas were to do eighty-six years later, Zelaya's government in Bluefields blamed the Miskito's continuing resistance not on territorial defense, but on the Moravian church for having been "always unfriendly and even openly hostile toward the Nicaraguan government" and for having "taught...the natives to disregard and disrespect the laws and customs of the country."[9]

Nine decades of Nicaraguan governments produced almost nothing except exports. "Reincorporation" for Nicaraguan governments meant access to valuable resources and cheap labor to profit western Nicaragua, and national and foreign business interests. "Reincorporation" for the Miskito, Sumo and Rama nations meant the disruption of national and regional Indian government and autonomy and the temporary transfer and camouflage of these centuries-old institutions into village-level politics and economics. During the Zelaya-through-Somoza occupations, the Miskito nation survived by decentralization of its institutions.

Occupation under the Somoza dictatorships

During the Somoza dictatorships (1935-1979), Miskito oppo-

23

sition was widespread to the seizure and export of their resources and the almost complete lack of reinvestment into or development of Miskito communities. But Managua maintained a very low political and military profile and most of the resource exploitation was in the hands of foreign companies, especially those from the United States and Canada. And these companies paid good wages and provided inexpensive imported goods and clothes, mostly from the United States.

The Miskito worked with foreign lumber and gold companies, adapted cash to reciprocity economies to support village life, and lived as best they could independent of the Somoza governments in Managua. Foreign companies largely supported the region's monetary economy, and the Moravian, Catholic and Anglican churches provided western education, medical supplies and health facilities. The Miskito, Sumo and Rama communities were still functionally autonomous due to the buffer of the rain forest and rain-drenched humid lowlands, and the Somoza dictatorships' strategy of acquiring maximum profits from minimum presence.

Resistance to territorial intrusion and to worker exploitation occurred frequently. For example, the Miskito organized several labor strikes in the gold mines and pine lumbering areas, and Miskito fishermen stopped catching lobster and sea turtles to pressure foreign companies to increase the amounts they paid for these valuable exports. Also in the early 1970s, Miskito turtlemen fought Jamaican fishermen and sabotaged fish traps set in Miskito territorial waters, which forced Managua and the National Guard to intervene and eventually to withdraw the Jamaicans' fishing permits. A decade before the Sandinistas took power, the Miskito organized a military force in reaction to the state's military occupation of their territory and forced relocation of Miskito people. The northern one-third of the Miskito nation was given to Honduras through Nicaragua's acceptance of a 1960 World Court decision. The

Miskito were not part of the international hearings that split their nation between two states. Honduras sent military units into "La Mosquitia"—renamed Departamento Cabo Gracias a Dios—to consolidate its claim.

Prior to 1960, the fertile Wangki River had united Miskito people who lived on and farmed both sides for hundreds of miles. With Honduras's assertion of sovereignty, the river—called the Río Coco in Spanish—became an international boundary that divided the Miskito nation. Brutal treatment by the Honduran army forced thousands of Miskito to cross the river as refugees who never returned home. In 1962-63 international aid helped build new settlements for the refugees (called *los traslados*) at Kiwastara, San Jerónimo, El Carmen, San Alberto, Santa Fe, La Esperanza and Santa Isabel on the south side of the Wangki, and at Santa Marta halfway along the Waspam-Bilwi (Puerto Cabezas) road.

The Honduran army repeatedly burned crops to force people to abandon settlement and subsistence use on the north side of the Wangki. The army also did at least two documented machine-gun sprayings of the traslado communities.

When war broke out between El Salvador and Honduras in July 1969 (the "Soccer War"), about 500 Miskito armed with hunting rifles, shotguns and machetes decided to take advantage of the distraction of the Salvadoran army's attacks on Honduran positions, and to cross the Wangki to attack Honduran army outposts and retake Miskito territory. Accidental discovery by a two-man Nicaraguan National Guard unit led to panicked communications with Managua and a hasty attempt to dissuade the Miskito force from bringing Nicaragua into the El Salvador-Honduras war. The Miskito force reluctantly did not attack.

Twenty years after Honduras's army invaded to assert state sovereignty over Miskito territory by burning crops and forcing thousands to cross the river to refugee communities, the Sandinista army would do the same thing.

25

The Miskito have never lived in splendid isolation; their nation has been under siege for almost 500 years.

The Sandinista occupation

To the Yapti Tasba nations, Sandinista Nicaragua is a superpower that has invaded their territory, taken their resources, and now occupies their communities.

To the west an urban guerrilla war by the FSLN and the Ladino people overthrew the Somoza dictatorship, 19 July 1979. The Sandinistas then came eastward to "liberate" the Indians and Creoles and their resources. The first Sandinista comandante to arrive in Bilwi was Manuel Calderón (Comandante "Rufo"), who spoke to several thousand Miskito in the Central Park on 21 July 1979:

> You Indians have been marginalized and exploited for more than forty years by the Somoza dictatorship. Somoza became a millionaire by exploiting your forest, sea and mining resources. As vanguard of the people, the FSLN has a special interest in the proletariat, campesinos, workers, Indians, youth and others. We will construct hospitals, clinics, schools. There will be scholarships for Indians. No longer will there be unemployment on the Atlantic Coast. There will be freedom of speech, freedom of religion in all of Nicaragua [translated from notes made by a Miskito student].

uses
real
peoples
opinion

A Miskito leader who is now in exile in Costa Rica, remarked on this "invasion by promises": "The Sandinistas spoke in the name of the people, for the poor, for the marginalized, for the exploited, for the humble. That was us. They were the vanguard of the people. The people now ruled Nicaragua. In the name of the people they took power. But after two months there was none of this people stuff. They were the government. They said they were our government."

Within three months the Sandinistas had imposed their CDS

bribery.

(Comités de Defensa Sandinista) surveillance network to ration food and to report on "counterrevolutionary activities," denied requests for a native language literacy campaign, killed Miskito activist Lester Athers, nationalized all land not covered by private ownership titles, and were cutting lumber from Miskito and Sumo communal lands.

U.S.-educated Sandinista Comandante Luis Carrión, then FSLN Directorate representative for the "Atlantic Coast," provided this analysis of the "indigenous problem":

The indigenous communities remember the Spanish through their oral tradition, only in terms of their unsuccessful attempts to conquer and subdue them. This is how we have here some tribes with their own language, their own culture, and with a very primitive social organization which is different from that of the rest of the country.

They do not feel themselves identified with the rest of the nation [state] and they continue to call all those who are not indigenous "Spanish" as they have done for a hundred years. The problem is then of a minority with its own particularities, and also with a great ideological backwardness. They claim the right to their own language, they claim the right to possess communal property and they claim participation in the administration which they say will be controlled by themselves. They live in a state of development still based on communal property, that is to say, there has never occurred a massive decomposition of communal land property, so they cultivate their lands as a community. There is no parcelization and they want their communities to be recognized legally as the property of one extension of land (*Barricada*, 6-7 May 1981).

In other words, the Indian peoples had their own distinct

national systems of identity, economy and property that were different from those of the Sandinista invaders. What the Sandinistas saw as "the Indian Problem," the Miskitos saw as "the Sandinista Problem." Limited by class-based Marxism, the Sandinistas have been unable to comprehend an identity and a resistance based on culture. Culture and homeland unify a people more strongly than do ideology, class, or adherence to a particular political-economic system or group of leaders.

In April 1985 when he assumed command of the FSLN occupation forces, Minister of Interior Tomás Borge went to Bluefields where he said: "Here there are no whites, blacks, Miskitos or Creoles. Here there are revolutionary and counterrevolutionary Nicaraguans, regardless of the color of their skin. The only thing that differentiates us is the attitude we assume toward the nation [state]."[10]

To create what the Sandinistas called a "New Indian," they tried to get the Indian peoples to join FSLN organizations imported from the West Coast. A Miskito youth leader remarked, "The Sandinistas said that the people were in power now and should organize. But Sandinista organizations weren't Indian organizations. We organized our own." Indian leaders moved to expand and restructure ALPROMISU (Alianza Para el Progreso de los Miskito y Sumu, founded in 1974) for Indian goals and to represent Indian interests to the FSLN. A General Assembly was held 8-11 November 1979 in Bilwi and 805 leaders attended, made up mostly of two delegates from each of the 256 indigenous communities. Against Sandinista objections, the Assembly founded Misurasata (Unity of Miskito, Sumo, Rama and Sandinista), and presented an agenda to guarantee communal land rights; rights to the mines and lumber on Indian lands; the need for Miskito, Sumo, Rama and English languages in the FSLN's Spanish "literacy campaign" (learn the invader's language); and the demand that the body of Lester Athers be returned from the

FSLN military base in Bilwi and that his FSLN killers be brought to trial. A directorate was formed with Stedman Fagoth, Brooklyn Rivera and Hazel Lau, and an executive committee with Alejo Teofilo, Wycliff Diego, Teodoro Downs and Roger Herman. Armstrong Wiggins was selected as the Misurasata representative in the Casa del Gobierno in Managua.

Only fifteen months later, all of these people (except Hazel Lau) would be arrested by the Sandinistas, and before its second anniversary Misurasata was banned by the FSLN and its leaders were political prisoners or in exile (Teodoro Downs spent twenty-three months in the maximum security prison El Chipote).

The FSLN brought their military, economic and political apparatus to the Indian and Creole nations in order to, in President Daniel Ortega's words, "rescue them and incorporate them" into the revolution.[11] For the Sandinistas, the Indians would be "revolutionary" if they relinquished their nationality, territory, resources, culture, history, government, and control over their own lives and future to become Nicaraguan campesinos led by the Sandinista vanguard. If Indian peoples resisted this revolutionary "rescue" and "incorporation," they would be "counterrevolutionary" and subject to appropriate measures to deal with "enemies of the state."

Sandinista organizations were imposed on the peoples of Yapti Tasba to control food production and distribution (ENABAS), labor (CTS, ATC), women (AMNLAE), resources (IRENA), land (INRA), education (MED), youth (JS 19), and, to make doubly sure, the FSLN sent more of their army (EPS), militia (MPS), air force (FAS), and state security (DGSE) forces.

At the same time Misurasata worked to organize Indian communities. Most of this grassroots organization was done by young Miskito men and women in Juventud Misurasata, and later, by Miskito literacy brigadistas. Reminiscing about the early days of Misurasata, Enerio Danny, an exiled Mis-

29

Miskito opinion voice

kito leader, told me: "The Piri [short for Pirikauku, rabid dog, the Miskito's name for the Sandinistas] thought we were going village to village teaching about Carlos Fonseca, Fidel Castro and Karl Marx, but we weren't interested in that junk. We talked about our land, our interests and our own leaders."

Misurasata and Sandinista leaders met in August 1980 in Managua to discuss the problem of state claims to Indian lands and resources. An agreement was reached whereby Misura would carry out a cadastral mapping and land tenure study of community lands which would be presented to the FSLN directorate by February 1981.

To hire surveyors to map the lands, special collections were taken during weekly church services, some village people sold jewelry, and Cultural Survival, an indigenous rights organization in Boston, Massachusetts, provided a small grant. A call went out to the communities to bring their land titles and maps to the Misurasata office in Bilwi where the land tenure project was being compiled. These titles and maps had been provided to each community by the British from 1860 to 1890 and they had been carefully guarded and protected during the following decades. Old men and women came from each community to bring the 100-year-old parchment maps and titles —their community's guarantee of land rights, and they demanded promises of safe-keeping from the Misurasata staff in Bilwi. Part of the project was to assemble a composite map from the individual community maps, and then to field check the boundaries with the assistance of the surveyors. As the composite map was assembled, it became apparent to all that the gold mines, the pine, mahogany and cedar, and the richest agricultural areas were all on Miskito, Sumo and Rama lands, and that each community's lands bounded with another community's to form extensive, unbroken territories.

Meanwhile, Misurasata held its second General Assembly, 26-29 December 1980 in Bilwaskarma on the Wangki, to lay

What is left of a seven-person Miskito family. The husband and brothers have been killed or are disappeared.

out a plan for indigenous socioeconomic and political development in the general areas of indigenous politics, cooperatives, land rights, literacy in native languages, health and education. The Misurasata "Plan of Action 1981" was only drafted in outline form,[12] but the Sandinistas read into it a danger to their revolution and occupation and moved to clamp down on the indigenous rights movement. What upset the Sandinistas about Plan '81 (later to be called a CIA operation by the FSLN) were Misurasata's plans to: 1) help promote an indigenous federation with the Subtiava and Momimbó peoples on the Pacific coast, 2) organize independent (non-FSLN) trade and workers unions for Indian mine workers, farmers and fishermen, and 3) begin "an intensive consciousness-raising campaign at the community level to prepare the political conditions for the handing over of the documents [land tenure map and 145-page land tenure study] to the authorities."

The FSLN saw Plan '81 and the mapping of Indian lands as threats to imposing their revolution on the occupied territories. Starting 19 February 1981, nine days before the land tenure map and study were to be presented to the FSLN directorate, Misurasata leaders were arrested in Managua and the mining region by Sandinista military and security personnel. At 6:15 P.M., 20 February, Sandinista soldiers surrounded and broke into the Misurasata office in Bilwi and hit Miskito boys and girls and men and women with rifle butts. Files were taken from the office and burned. The officer in charge told the people they held captive: "You are counter-revolutionaries, separatists, somocistas, CIA agents. You have ten minutes to live." At 9:00 P.M., forty-five miles to the south, at Prinsapolka, Sandinista soldiers broke into the Moravian church during a religious ceremony to arrest Elmer Prado, a Misurasata official. A scuffle occurred, a Sandinista officer shot Prado in the hand with a Galil automatic rifle, and many Miskito boys rushed to Prado's defense. Four armed Sandinistas and four unarmed Miskito were killed. The war had started. Sandinista military units went from village to village arresting Miskito literacy campaign workers and members of Misurasata. Within a few days hundreds of Miskito were in hiding and thousands were converging on Waspam, the mines and Bilwi to protest the arrest of their leaders. Within the next six months 5000 Miskito and Sumo—mostly young men and teen-age boys—and almost all the leaders were in Honduras. They sought military assistance.

During August through October 1981 some sixty-five young men received training from Comandante "Bravo" (ex-National Guard) and two Argentine military instructors. No arms were provided, although they were promised some FAL automatic rifles. Finally, some uniforms and boots were received but a severe dispute occurred with Steadman Fagoth over his heavy-handed leadership, and the first group quit on the spot, left their boots and uniforms on the ground and headed for the Wangki. This almost legendary group of sixty-five young Miskito and Sumo was named "Los Astros."

The Astros slipped across the Wangki and obtained some .22 rifles and shotguns from willing Miskito villagers. About 80 percent of the group was armed with machetes, knives and bows and arrows. Their objective was to liberate the Indian communities and territory from Sandinista occupation. Their plan was to strike at the small garrisons of Sandinista soldiers in the Wangki villages, recover weapons, pick up Miskito recruits, train them in the bush, and using larger and larger forces, move southward to drive the Sandinistas from the East Coast.

In late November the Astros made surprise hit-and-run raids against Sandinista EPS and DGSE outposts on the Wangki at Santa Isabel, Krasa, Kuabul, El Gamalote, Wani, Bluno, and Asang, moving community to community up the river. By mid-December one-half of the group was armed with AK-47s, a FAL, and some M-16s, all recovered from Sandinis-

33

tas. On 18 December, with the help of Miskito civilians, the Astros overran an EPS garrison at San Carlos, shot down a helicopter and captured many weapons. But on 23 December, the Sandinistas mounted a serious counterattack with air support and the Astros barely managed to hold off the ESP troops long enough for most of the San Carlos people to escape across the Wangki. The DGSE arrested forty civilians and the EPS strengthened the garrison.

Militarily, the attacks on the EPS outposts and garrisons by the Astros were unsuccessful; the Sandinistas counterattacked, often killing civilians, EPS and DGSE forces were increased in numbers and armaments, and the DGSE made widespread arbitrary arrests. Politically, however, the Astro attacks represented the first blow against the despised Sandinista occupation. It was the beginning of organized military resistance against the occupation.

To deal with the sixty-five-member Astros, the Sandinistas began to forcibly relocate thousands of people and to burn down the Wangki villages. The destruction of the Wangki began in late December 1981 and expanded to include Miskito communities to the south and the Sumo nation during 1982. In the first months of 1982, sixty-five Wangki communities (one for each Astro) had been leveled, 10,000 Miskito were held in Sandinista relocations camps, and another 10,000 had fled across the Wangki as refugees. The Sandinistas had committed an act of war by destroying the heartland of the Miskito nation.

The Sandinistas treated the Indian and Creole defensive war against them as an insurgency and they used standard counterinsurgency tactics: more forced relocations and arrests, disappearances, theft, confiscation and expropriation of almost everything of value, destruction of more villages—some by bomb and rocket attacks, control of food and medicine, military occupation of villages to intimidate the people, creation of a puppet government and a conscription of coast people to fight against the resistance, development of a network of informers and infiltrators, and replacement of local institutions with those of the occupiers (*Table* 1, p. 36).

The Miskito bore the brunt of the fighting and development of political objectives. Rama, Sumo and Creole fighters made critical contributions throughout the war. The three main resistance organizations (Misurasata, Misura and Kisan) formed Yatama, a single unified force in June 1987 at the Third General Assembly held in Rus Rus, in the northern part of the Miskito nation claimed by Honduras.

The Indian defensive struggle against the Sandinista occupation government and army progressed rapidly. From a grassroots land rights movement in 1979, Misurasata attracted so much Indian political support that it became the effective government by 1980. Outlawed in 1981, the Indian rights movement opened up a military resistance, which split in 1982 into Misurasata and Misura. Inside occupied Indian nations the resistance groups fought as one and represented the only Indian army in the Americas. By the end of 1983 the 6000 fighters controlled most of their national territory. They had won major victories, including those at Seven Benk, Corn River, La Tronquera, Gunpoint, and Haulover, and they had destroyed Soviet T-55 tanks, the main FSLN fuel installation (amphibious attack), and one-half of the Puerto Cabezas wharf (frogman attack).

Most of the armed Indian resistance force operated permanently within the four Yapti Tasba nations, a 400- by 200-kilometer front. At all times there were more volunteers than arms. Recruits were given training at the many secret base camps scattered throughout Yapti Tasba. The armed resistance had the capability of adding another 10,000 fighters but could not due to limitations imposed by ARDE, the FDN and the CIA.

The Indian-Sandinista war is one of the major armed conflicts in Latin America in recent decades, ranking fourth in

35

TABLE 1.
Sandinista Occupation Policies, 1979-1988

1979 Invasion under the mantle of liberation; the beginning of annexation of resources and land; establishment of FSLN institutions to control coast society and economy; attempts subjugate Indian leadership.

1980 Expansion of FSLN military; attempts to seize resources; confrontations with communities; attempts to subjugate and bypass Misurasata.

1981 Consolidation by mass arrests of Misurasata leaders and followers; demonstration at Prinsapolka of willingness to use weapons without provocation; outlawing of Misurasata; forced exile of Indian leaders; large-scale military invasion and crackdown, the Leimus Massacre, Wangki village burnings.

1982 Destruction of Indian villages; forced relocation of civilians into the first of thirteen state camps; state of siege against Indian peoples; widespread arrests by DGSE; displacement of 20 percent of the coast peoples; fabrication of external threats ("Red Christmas") to justify use of military force against civilians.

1983 Arbitrary brutality by military and security forces to crack down and terrorize Indian civilians into submission and to stop their support of Indian resistance fighters; 30 percent of people displaced.

1984 Emergence of new occupation policy to gain control by expansion of puppet government and conscription of coast people into Sandinista army and security forces; FSLN creation of their Indian organization MISATAN; first negotiation with Misurasata to obtain cease-fire but without landrights; 40 percent of people now displaced.

1985 Break-off of negotiations; start of long-range "hearts and minds" strategy and centralization of the occupation under Minister of Interior Tomás Borge; negotiation of some cease-fires with individual Indian resistance units; promotion of FSLN autonomy plan.

1986 Large-scale improvement of rapid deployment of upgraded military and security forces; MI-17 and MI-24 helicopters, better communications, more patrol boats; withdrawal of army from some villages to main bases; closing of some relocation camps; "autonomy" campaign.

1987 Manipulation of food scarcity; special anti-guerrilla "BLI" and "Cazador" army units; "autonomy" law passed.

1988 Negotiations with Yatama in effort to absorb political and military resistance; Hurricane "Joan" devastates southern Yapti Tasba; Cuban military forces brought in.

intensity behind the three insurgency wars in Nicaragua, El Salvador and Guatemala. Sandinista occupation forces have targeted Indian communities in an attempt to cut civilian support (food, shelter, information, recruits) to the Indian resistance (*Map* 4, p. 38).

Allies who share only enemies

The location of the Miskito nation on Nicaragua's third border, its sea access, its extensive forests and complex topography, and its peoples' historical resistance against invaders, provided critical advantages for it to sustain guerrilla (low intensity) warfare. The Sandinistas attacked a nation of hunters and seamen whose experience and skills were quickly converted by Miskito nationalists into the basis of a resistance force. Miskito leaders sought outside assistance based on the old Arab proverb, "the enemy of my enemy is my arms supplier." This meant trying to equip and maintain a several thousand man guerrilla force by soliciting supplies even from other organizations that were antagonistic to Indian nationalistic aspirations.

While proclaiming great differences between their organizations, ARDE and the FDN were in total agreement over Indian autonomy and weapons: block autonomy and block formation of a well-equipped Indian army. Indian fighters were allowed only a trickle of light weapons in an effort to limit them to ambushes that would tie up and spread out thousands of Sandinista soldiers. But ARDE and the FDN did not want Indian military forces to win an overall victory or even to gain territorial control over everything outside the two coast cities (both were very possible in 1983-1984). ARDE leaders Edén Pastora and Alfonso Robelo and FDN (now Resistencia Nicaragüense) leaders Adolfo Calero and Enríque Bermúdez feared the untapped military and political potential of the Indian resistance and did not want to see a well-equipped Indian army that they might have to face some day when

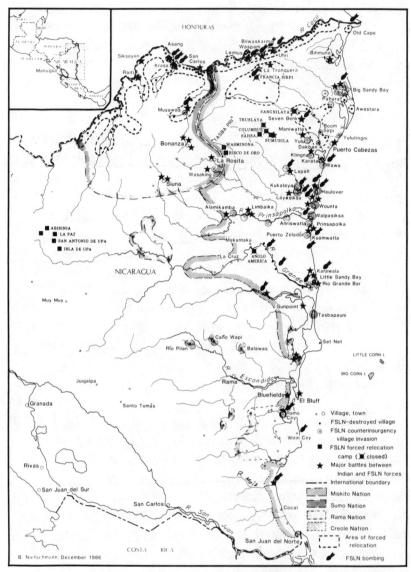

HONDURAS

Old Cape

Asang
Bilwaskarma
Waspam
Siksayari
Leimus
Uhri
Bihmuna
San
Carlos
Krasa
La Tronquera
Raiti
FRANCIA SIRPI
Big Sandy Bay
Pahara
Musawas
Awastara
SANGNILAYA
TRUSLAYA
Seven Benk
Boom
COLUMBUS
Maniwatla
Sirpi
SAHSA
Yulutingni
Bonanza
SUMUBILA
Yulu
WASMINONA
Dakban
Puerto Cabezas
RISCO DE ORO
Klingna
La Rosita
Karata
Wawa
Lapan
Wasaking
Siuna
Kukalaya
Layasiksa
Haulover
Alamikamba
Limbaika
Wounta
R. Prinsapolka
Anriswatla
Walpasiksa
ABISINIA
Prinsapolka
LA PAZ
Puerto Zelado
Kuamwatla
SAN ANTONIO DE UPA
Makantaka
ISLA DE UPA
La Cruz
ANGLO
AMERICA
NICARAGUA
Karawala
Little Sandy Bay
Rio Grande Bar
Muy Muy
Gunpoint
Tasbapauni
Caño Wapi
Set Net
Río Pilan
Balawas
LITTLE CORN I.
BIG CORN I.
Juigalpa
Rama
R. Escondido
Granada
Bluefields
El Bluff
Santo Tomás
Village, town
Rama
FSLN–destroyed village
Cay
FSLN counterinsurgency
Wirin Cay
village invasion
Rivas
FSLN forced relocation
camp (✖ closed)
Major battles between
Indian and FSLN forces
San Juan del Sur
International boundary
San Carlos
Cocal
Miskito Nation
R. San Juan
Sumo Nation
Rama Nation
Creole Nation
Area of forced
relocation
San Juan del Norte
COSTA RICA
B. Nietschmann, December 1986
FSLN bombing

MAP 4   INDIAN-SANDINISTA CONFLICTS

their Managua government moved to "integrate" the coast. Even though they shared the same FSLN enemy, the 1982-85 relationship between Misurasata and ARDE, and Misura and the FDN was often hostile and always acrimonious. Indian comandantes talked about a near-future "third war" if the contras should ever take power in Managua and try to invade the coast.

CIA objectives were to assist the Indian resistance organizations to the extent that they broadened the conflict against the FSLN. The nationalistic aspirations of the Indian peoples were seen as a side issue that not only inflamed ARDE and FDN leaders but threatened the establishment of a united front against the Sandinistas. Put off by the territorial goals of the Indian resistance forces, the CIA nevertheless recognized that the Indians were far and away the best fighters, and for this reason they were given some arms and supplies.

CIA support to Honduras-based Misura was at first channeled through the FDN but political friction led by late 1982 to direct deliveries of supplies and arms. The amounts were small. To the south, Misurasata had to work to pry even old weapons and motors from ARDE people who had ample unused quantities of brand new automatic weapons, grenade and rocket launchers, light machine guns, and outboard motors. But with old Soviet BCA rifles and undependable outboard motors, Misurasata's fighters seized effective control of the southern one-half of Yapti Tasba, from Wounta to Monkey Point. The CIA reasoned that if these fighters could do that with hand-me-down weapons, they could really do some damage with good equipment. Misurasata received a shipment of 200 "equipos" (arms and full equipment) during October 1984. More were promised. With their first good weapons, the Misurasata fighters went on the offensive and effectively liberated all of the area between Bluefields and Puerto Cabezas.

But these military successes were short lived. In December

1984, Misurasata entered into negotiations with the FSLN, which produced confusion and consternation among the Indian commanders and fighters. The 1984-85 negotiations led only to the blockade of further distribution of arms to Misurasata fighters in central and southern Yapti Tasba who desperately needed them to defend against Sandinista forces trained by Cuban combat veterans from Angola and equipped with excellent Soviet weapons, helicopters, communications and intelligence.

Arms distribution to Misura and Kisan (formed in October 1985) continued, although on a small scale. Nevertheless, fighters from these organizations were able to force the upgraded Sandinista occupation army to a military stalemate. In 1986 Misurasata commanders bypassed political leader Brooklyn Rivera and took their demands for more arms directly to U.S. representatives.

The Indian resistance organizations wanted arms, communications, boats and money from the CIA. The CIA wanted unification with the contras, coordination and "accountability." The CIA condemned "Indian politics" as being militarily disruptive. The Indian leaders condemned poor CIA logistical support as the cause for lags in fighting.

Friction increased and by early 1987 dangerous tension existed between the CIA's "cowboys" and Indian political and military leaders. In Washington, the U.S. State Department challenged the CIA on its handling of support to Misurasata, Misura and Kisan, and managed to wrest from Langley the authority over the $5 million appropriated by Congress as part of the 1986 $100 million contra aid package. The U.S. State Department's Nicaragua Coordinating Office (NCO) had responsibility for approving budgetary requests.

One of the first requests was for a General Assembly of representatives from Yapti Tasba communities, refugee communities and the three resistance organizations. In June 1987 some 2000 Yapti Tasba people met in Rus Rus (Honduras) and united Misurasata, Misura and Kisan into one organization called Yatama. Four people were selected to Yatama's directorate—three Miskitos: Brooklyn Rivera, Wycliff Diego, and Steadman Fagoth, and Charley Morales, a Sumo. A Creole and Rama leader were to be named later.

During the summer and fall of 1987, Indian fighters received quantities of good weapons and equipment for the first time in the war. With these, Yatama units launched a series of attacks against the Sandinista military in the occupied territories and destroyed the FSLN's main radar installation just north of Puerto Cabezas, paralyzed military transport, and began to seal off Puerto Cabezas. Even though these were the most effective operations of the war, they were not reported by the international press. But the Sandinistas had been hit hard and even their elite "BLI" and "Cazador" anti-guerrilla units were on the defensive.

It was at this time that Yatama's Brooklyn Rivera tried to parlay these military successes into a negotiated settlement with the Sandinistas. President Oscar Arias, who had just engineered the Esquipulas II peace plan, said he would support a peace initiative between Yatama and the FSLN. In the fall of 1987, at the height of Yatama's military build-up, Rivera and Nicaragua's Minister of Interior Tomás Borge agreed to another round of negotiations. Internally, Rivera fought to convince others to go with him to Managua and cited supposed State Department and CIA foul-ups and manipulations as the reasons for being "pushed" into negotiations. Scheduled for October but put off due to the FSLN's arrogant preconditions, negotiations were begun in late January 1988. This was the second time that Rivera had taken U.S. military aid and then entered into negotiations with the FSLN. The State Department was exasperated with Rivera's turnaround.

The decision to negotiate again with the FSLN led to a series of major setbacks for Yatama: 1) Yatama fighters withdrew from large areas taken during the Fall '87 assault, allow-

41

ing the Sandinistas to regroup; 2) divisions widened in Yatama between advocates of military and advocates of political solutions to the FSLN occupation; 3) the 2 February 1988 FSLN-Yatama Preliminary Accords gave a false impression that peace was at hand, which led to the narrow defeat in Washington on 3 February of more U.S. military assistance, sidelined many Yatama guerrilla units, and took international pressure off the Sandinistas; and 4) some Yatama military commanders signed individual peace agreements which cut back military strength and weakened Yatama's negotiating leverage.

The negotiations failed to produce even one positive gain for Yatama, except to demonstrate that the FSLN was intransigent and unwilling to make any concessions that would end the war with Yapti Tasba.

The politics of refugees
The Sandinista war and military occupation displaced approximately 70,000 Yapti Tasba people, one-fourth of the population. Some 50,000 fled to fourteen other countries as refugees and exiles; 20,000 became "internal" refugees in other communities and in the Sandinista relocation camps.

The refugee situation in Honduras is a tragedy. From the beginning in 1982, the UNHCR-administered camps have not provided adequate food, medicine, shelter or clothing. In 1986, in the northern Miskito nation (eastern Honduras) there were 30,000 Miskito and Sumo in eighteen UNHCR refugee camps and 10,000 others who had left the impoverished camps to live precariously but independently on the "Honduran" side of the Wangki. Isolation, poor transportation, and budget restrictions account for some of the disastrous conditions, but the fundamental problem continues to be UNHCR efforts to force "repatriation" to Nicaragua. The FSLN has issued a series of "amnesties" beginning in December 1983 to get the Indian resistance and refugees to return. The UNHCR forces repatria-

Miskito refugee, Honduras. Many people have spent seven years living in such difficult conditions.

tion based on these FSLN amnesty promises. To get the refugees to repatriate, the UNHCR began a "carrot and stick" policy in 1984: give 150 lempira (U.S. $75.00) per person and free transportation to those who would go to Nicaragua, and cut back on food and material assistance to those who don't want to return to Nicaragua. As a result, in 1984-86 some 10,000 people left the camps because of UNHCR economic repression.

The living conditions for all of the refugees in Honduras are so difficult that many left to return to their burned-down communities, especially along the Wangki down river from Waspam. In March 1988 the people of Kum, Wasla and Saupuka told the Yatama negotiation delegation that they preferred to take their chances, even die, on their own land rather than to sit in the mud in refugee camps and be abused by the UNHCR and the Honduran occupation army and government. Though they had not received material assistance from the FSLN or the International Red Cross, these people had made a valiant start rebuilding their communities and lives. Some 5000 Yapti Tasba refugees are in Costa Rica. Approximately 80 percent are not in refugee camps but are living in Caribbean coast communities or in and around San José. About 1000 are in refugee camps, mainly the Pueblo Nuevo camp on the outskirts of the Caribbean port of Limón.

Costa Rica's efforts to end some of the wars in Central America with a regional peace plan (Esquipulas II) have failed to produce anything but more refugees from Nicaragua and Yapti Tasba. Refugees are a political liability for President Oscar Arias and an economic drain on the Costa Rican economy. Therefore, Nicaraguan and Yapti Tasba refugees are pressured to "repatriate." This is being done by reducing food allotments in the Pueblo Nuevo camp, revoking fishing permits given to Yapti Tasba refugees, and promoting the UNHCR repatriation program that includes a cash payment of U.S. $75.00 for signing up to leave.

More refugees and exiles from Nicaragua and Yapti Tasba will come to Honduras, Costa Rica and other countries because of Sandinista repression and economic mismanagement, the failure of the Esquipulas II peace initiative, and most recently the devastation caused by Hurricane "Joan" (22-23 October 1988), the Sandinistas' politically selective distribution of emergency assistance and massive influx of Cuban soldiers and Cuban militarization of Yapti Tasba.

Between Nicaragua and Cuba
Strategic interests don't simply take place, they take place in a place. Yapti Tasba has great strategic importance because of its location, its resources and its history of military resistance.

Control of Yapti Tasba is vital to the Sandinistas. Yapti Tasba lies between Sandinista Nicaragua and Cuba. Under their military occupation it is the front door to Cuba and to the Soviet Union and key to domination of critical sea lanes. It is one of the main areas the Sandinistas plan to hold onto in case they are forced from power in Managua.

Sandinista military buildup in Yapti Tasba has been extensive and demonstrates a commitment to annex the territories and to use them to project a Sandinista presence into the Caribbean (*Map* 5, p. 46). The Sandinistas have built MIG-ready airfields in Puerto Cabezas and Bluefields and they have recently extended and improved a forward operations airfield in Waspam close to Honduran and U.S. military bases. A sophisticated radar installation, Soviet Mi-24 helicopter gunships, Mi-17 helicopter troop carriers, chemical spray equipped AN-2 biplanes, and Special Forces units are based in Puerto Cabezas. Soviet Komar-class naval vessels are based in Puerto Cabezas and at El Bluff. Port facilities at El Bluff have been upgraded extensively to handle heavy Soviet shipments of arms, armor and artillery destined for Managua and the occupied territories. The capacity for naval surface craft and submarines

45

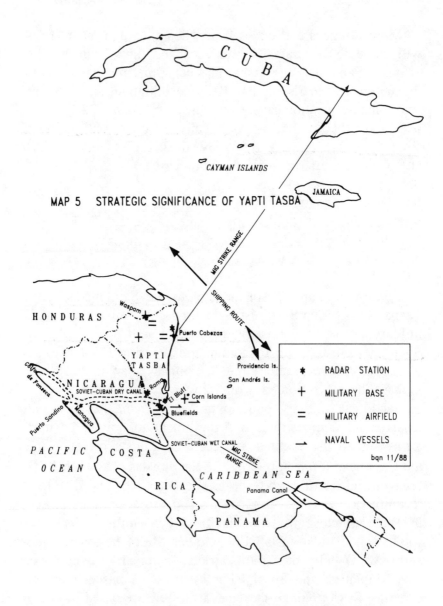

MAP 5   STRATEGIC SIGNIFICANCE OF YAPTI TASBA

✳	RADAR STATION
+	MILITARY BASE
=	MILITARY AIRFIELD
→	NAVAL VESSELS

bqn 11/88

MAP 5 STRATEGIC SIGNIFICANCE OF YAPTI TASBA

has been enhanced through extensive dredging and construction of seawalls and breakwaters. El Bluff is the Caribbean gateway to the planned "dry canal" that will give the Soviets and Cubans their own inter-oceanic transport across Nicaragua to Puerto Sandino.

On 22 October 1988 Hurricane "Joan" critically damaged Sandinista military installations at El Bluff, Bluefields and Corn Island, filled in dredged channels, and caused landslides that closed the Rama Road. Within three days, the first Cuban detachments of military-construction forces were airlifted to Bluefields and Corn Island. Cuban naval vessels were sent to replace those destroyed at El Bluff and Corn Island by the hurricane.

Cuban strategic interest in Yapti Tasba is demonstrated by the speed, size and nature of their military deployment response. Several contingents of Cuban soldiers and military-construction personnel worked to reconstruct and enlarge hurricane-destroyed bases and airfields. The expanded bases and airfields and Cuban military presence are well beyond what the FSLN needs to maintain its occupation of Yapti Tasba. Clearly, the new military facilities and second occupation army mean: 1) that Cuba has decided to have an expanded presence in Central America, and 2) the FSLN is preparing to spread into the Caribbean.

The Cuban-Sandinista militarization of Yapti Tasba establishes Managua's and Havana's capacity to close off the western Caribbean and its vital shipping lanes and to expand a shadow of intimidation across Jamaica, Costa Rica and Honduras. Yapti Tasba is now serving as a base for Cuban soldiers, Mi-24 helicopters, MIG-ready airfields and pilots, and Soviet naval vessels.

The Sandinistas plan to pay off some of their international debts and obtain much needed hard cash by selling the natural resources of the occupied territories. Valuable and abundant reserves exist of mahogany, cedar, other tropical hardwoods and Caribbean lowland pine, gold and other minerals, shrimp and lobster, and petroleum. The presence of an oil field—possibly an important one—was confirmed during the Somoza occupation by exploratory offshore wells in 1978 (*Map* 6, p. 49).

Indian America and Latin America
Latin America is also Indian America. The countries, resources and nationalities of several hundred enduring nations are claimed by but twenty-two relatively new states and overseas territories even though the nation peoples have not relinquished sovereignty. Almost 500 years of regional hot and cold wars have resulted. The goal of conquest of the first nations and annexation of their lands, waters and resources has been attempted by invading colonialists, nationalists, capitalists, imperialists and, now, Marxists. But despite centuries of siege, many of the original nations and peoples persist and maintain their own distinct national territories and identities.

The reemergence of Indian America and the strengthening defense of the Indian peoples' nationalities, territories and resources have considerable regional and international geopolitical importance. This is especially true in Central America.

Traditional perspectives on Central America see seven states that are ruled by left-wing or right-wing dictatorships or oligarchies. Political analysts describe Central American peoples as prisoners of poverty or exploitation. They portray everyone as a member of one of the states (i.e. Guatemalan or Panamanian). They interpret Central America's peoples and aspirations in terms of class (workers and campesinos), political system (communism or democracy), and economic system (socialism or capitalism). Each view plays to a constituency, defines a condition, and promotes a solution: either bring the underclass up or the upperclass down.

Another view of Central America sees fifty enduring nations with a population of over 6 million people (23 percent

48

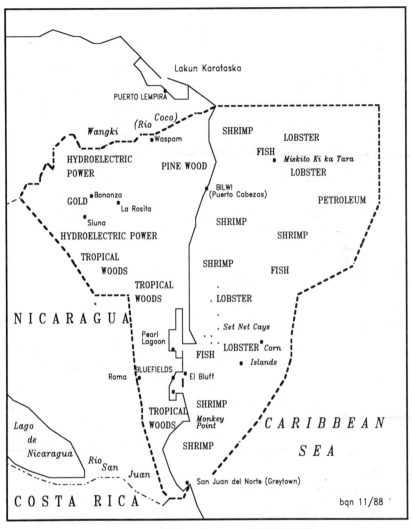

MAP 6 YAPTI TASBA RESOURCES

of Central America's population). Their countries have a combined area of more than 207,120 square kilometers, or 40 percent of all of Central America. The more than 5 million people in the twenty-two Maya nations (inside Guatemala) form a larger population than any Central American state.

If one looks at Central America in terms of the geographic limits to effective state government control, rather than unilateral claims of sovereignty, the region has a different geopolitical appearance (*Map* 7, p. 51). Viewed this way several significant geopolitical realities normally hidden by assertions of state hegemony emerge. Mexico and Guatemala mostly border the Maya nations, not each other. Some 20 percent of the people described as Salvadoran "campesinos" are from the Pipil nation. Nicaragua has no Caribbean coast. The Guaymí nation separates Costa Rica and Panama. Panama controls but a small piece of its claimed Caribbean coastline. And Central America's wars mostly are being fought within the national territories of indigenous peoples.

The Kuna have an autonomous nation called Kuna Yala to the east of Panama's Caribbean coast. The Guaymí are now negotiating a similar status for their nation with the Panamanian government. The Miskito have the only Indian army in the Americas and they are acknowledged to be the best combatants in Central America. And the Maya nations are the key geographic buffer against the spread of the insurgency and central government repression in Guatemala.

Firebreak nations for geopolitical hot spots

Central America is rapidly emerging as a world region on a geopolitical par with Southeast Asia and the Middle East. It is one of the world's compression points where superpower interests, contending governments and insurgents, fast growing populations and collapsing economies, and land invasions and environmental destruction are imploding to create flashpoint conditions.

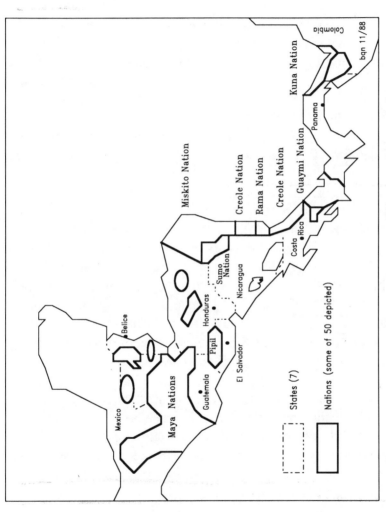

Mexico

Belice

Maya Nations

Miskito Nation

Guatemala

Honduras

Pipil

Sumo
Nation

El Salvador

Nicaragua

Creole Nation

Rama Nation

Creole Nation

Costa
Rica

Guaymi Nation

Panama

Kuna Nation

Colombia

bqn 11/88

States (7)

Nations (some of 50 depicted)

MAP 7   STATES AND NATIONS OF CENTRAL AMERICA

State-centered analyses of these conditions usually over-look the actual or potential role of Central America's original nations that collectively contain one-fourth of the population and almost one-half of the land. For example, the 1983 Kissinger Commission Report, a cornerstone of United States' Central American policy and Caribbean Basin initiative, does not even mention the Mayan peoples, or any other indigenous peoples in Central America.

Indigenous nations are a territorial and cultural firebreak to the spread of communism and other totalitarian regimes. In Latin America, communism has taken hold where there were no indigenous nations (Cuba and Grenada), and communism has been confronted and stymied where there are indigenous nations (Bolivia and Nicaragua).[13] In Cuba there were no indigenous peoples to resist communism because they had been killed off centuries before by Spanish colonialists. The same is true for Grenada, except it was the French and British colonial armies that finally destroyed the island's Carib people after more than 100 years of bitter war. But in Bolivia when Che Guevara tried to spread Castrismo communism to the highland indigenous nations, the Indian peoples turned their backs and Cuban expansion foundered and perished. And in Nicaragua—the first country in mainland America where Communists took control of a state government—it was the Miskito nation that was the first to rise up in arms to confront the Sandinistas.

Central state communism and indigenous nations are fundamentally incompatible. This is because each indigenous nation's politics, economics and society are inexorably tied to self-determination over its own territory and resource base. Nevertheless, Marxist academics and Eastern bloc advisors maintain a perpetual effort to explore ways to include the peoples of indigenous nations into "liberation movements." In Guatemala in the early 1980s, the leftist Poor People's Army (EGP) added thousands of Mayans to their ranks and became a major insurgent force by claiming the struggle was to drive whites off Indian land. (This is the same manipulative strategy Peru's *Sendero Luminoso* uses in its insurgency against the non-Indian government of an Indian country.) In Nicaragua, by mid-1984 the Sandinista leadership saw that their military strategy had not only failed to integrate the occupied territories, it had provoked the creation of an Indian army and solidified a grassroots resistance movement for autonomy. On the advice of Cuban and Soviet advisors and American and European academics, the Sandinistas decided to change their tactics from trying to crush the movement for autonomy to trying to redirect it. In December 1984 the FSLN created its own Autonomy Commission for the occupied territories and began talking about "Indian rights."

Real Indian rights to indigenous national territories and resources represent a real solution to escalating and expanding problems in Central America, Latin America in general and other world geopolitical hot spots. Without recognized territorial rights and without modern self-defense capabilities, the territories of many nations are used by outsiders for drug production and trafficking, environmentally destructive resource extraction, and wars between insurgents and state governments.

The "Firebreak Nation Theory" is based on four items: 1) the nation is structurally stronger and more resistant than the state because it is rooted in history, geography and culture; 2) many nations have persisted through centuries of siege and have not only withstood modern war, they are fighting the world's longest wars (Kurdistan, Eritrea, Kawthoolei, etc.); 3) many nations occupy strategic positions in explosive world regions; and 4) nations that persist, resist and have key locations are important potential firebreaks against the spread of totalitarian state regimes, insurgencies, drugs and environmental destruction.

The Miskito nation can block direct Cuban and Soviet access to Nicaragua and Sandinista expansion into the Caribbean. The

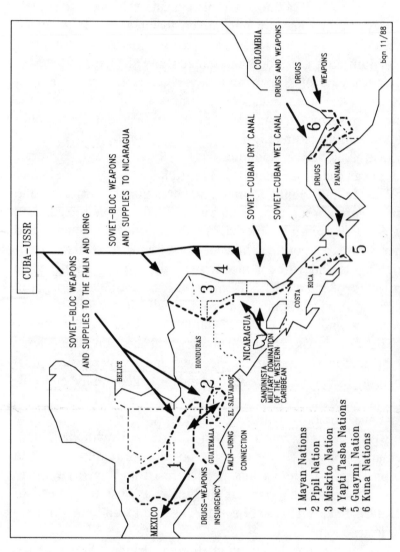

CUBA–USSR

SOVIET–BLOC WEAPONS
AND SUPPLIES TO THE FMLN AND URNG

SOVIET–BLOC WEAPONS
AND SUPPLIES TO NICARAGUA

SOVIET–CUBAN DRY CANAL

SOVIET–CUBAN WET CANAL

COLOMBIA

DRUGS AND WEAPONS

DRUGS

WEAPONS

6

DRUGS

PANAMA

5

COSTA

RICA

SANDINISTA
MILITARY DOMINATION
OF THE WESTERN
CARIBBEAN

NICARAGUA

3

4

HONDURAS

BELICE

2

EL SALVADOR

GUATEMALA

FMLN–URNG
CONNECTION

DRUGS–WEAPONS
INSURGENCY

MEXICO

1 Mayan Nations
2 Pipil Nation
3 Miskito Nation
4 Yapti Tasba Nations
5 Guaymi Nation
6 Kuna Nations

bqn 11/88

MAP 8   FIREBREAK NATIONS IN CENTRAL AMERICA

Kuna nation cuts across the Colombia-Panama cocaine trafficking route as does the Guaymí nation which is astride the Panama-Costa Rica connection. And the Mayan nations are located between Guatemala and Mexico, which in the near future may be an important neutral area between two potential politically explosive states (*Map* 8, p. 54).

Communism, insurgency conflicts, totalitarian state governments, drugs and survival-threatening deforestation can be contained and controlled more by territorial agreements between states and nations than by political agreements between states. This has potential not only in Central America, but elsewhere as well. The majority of the world's wars, refugees, genocide, human rights violations, environmental destruction and drug production occur on nation territories.[14] Fully 72 percent of the world's current 120 wars are between states and nations (Iraq vs. Kurdistan, Burma vs. Kawthoolei, Bangladesh vs. Chittagong Hill Tracts, Ethiopia vs. Eritrea, Indonesia vs. West Papua, Israel vs. Palestine, Nicaragua vs. Yapti Tasba, etc.). These represent conflicts over national territory, not over mere politics, ideology, religion, "ethnicity," or class.

Historically, the Miskito nation has been a territorial firebreak that contained Spain's colonialism and Nicaragua's nationalism. For the last ten years it has impeded the spread of the FSLN's Marxist-Leninism. And it has the potential of preventing a Cuban-Nicaraguan hegemony over the western Caribbean and much of Central America.

NOTES

1. Squier, George Ephraim, Waikna: *Adventures on the Mosquito Shore, 1852.*

2. Day, Peter, "Miskito Power," *Quadrant*, January-February, 1988, No. 241, Vol. 32, Nos. 1 & 2, pp. 27-37, Sydney, Australia.

3. Helms, Mary, *Asang: Adaptations to Culture Contact in a Miskito Community.* University of Florida Press, 1971.

4. Floyd, Troy S., *The Anglo-Spanish Struggle for Mosquitia.* University of New Mexico Press, 1967; Dozier, Craig L., *Nicaragua's Mosquito Shore.* University of Alabama Press, 1985.

5. Jenkins, Jorgé, *El Desafío Indígena en Nicaragua: El Caso de Los Miskitos,* Editorial Vanguardia, Managua, 1986.

6. Day, p. 31.

7. Day, p. 31.

8. Day, p 28.

9. Day, p. 29.

10. The *New York Times,* 26 April 1985.

11. Ortega, Daniel, Foreign Broadcast Information Service, Daily Reports, Washington, D.C., 19 November 1986, pp. 5-10.

12. "Misurasata, Plan of Action 1981," *National Revolution and Indigenous Identity,* Klaudine Ohland and Robin Schneider, eds., International Work Group for Indigenous Affairs, Document 47, Copenhagen, 1983, pp. 89-94.

13. Spadafora, Hugo and Bernard Nietschmann, "La Lucha de Los Indios de Nicaragua y La Comision Kissinger," *La Nación Internacional,* San José, Costa Rica, 7 June 1984, and *Las Derrotas Somocista y Comunista en Nicaragua,* a collection of writings of Dr. Hugo Spadafora, San José, Costa Rica, 1984, pp. 141-147.

14. Nietschmann, Bernard, "The Third World War," *Cultural Survival Quarterly,* Vol. 11, No. 2, pp. 1-16, 1987.

Negotiating with the Sandinistas

THE DUSTY SMUDGE that marked Managua was coming up fast. We had all been declared Enemies of the Revolution and in a couple of minutes we were going to land in the middle of that revolution. Glenn Morris (Shawnee attorney-advisor) threaded warrior beads onto his long braid. Brooklyn Rivera (Miskito Yatama coordinator) read over pages of notes written in his tight, neat script. Gringo attorney-advisor Steve Tullberg adjusted his blue blazer and red Washington "power tie." Jim Anaya (Mescalero Apache attorney-advisor) put away his Toshiba laptop. Miskito leader Julian Smith reached for the shopping bag filled with eight million *córdobas*, a left over from the Pastora days but now worth no more than taxi fares. Walter Ortiz (Rama leader) had been dozing but was now very wide awake. We banked over Managua and Jenelee Hodgson (Creole leader) and Herta Downs (Miskito leader) strained to see something familiar after so many years. Miskito leader and Yatama Ambassador Armstrong Wiggins closed his briefcase and winked at me. Modesto Watson, Marcos Hoppington and Samuel Mercado—the other leaders in the Yatama armed resistance—signaled that we should wait and get off as a group. And—gringo geographer-

Bernard Nietschmann?

advisor—I scribbled these last-minute impressions in my notebook.

Our Copa Flight 318 touched down in Sandinista Nicaragua at 6:05 P.M., 23 January 1988, with thirteen anti-Sandinista resistance leaders and advisors abroad. We didn't know if we would be welcomed or arrested. Just before we took off from San José, Costa Rica the Nicaraguan Ministry of Interior had sent orders that the plane would not be allowed to land in Managua if we were aboard. We hoped something had been worked out during the thirty-minute flight.

Glimpses of Soviet Mi-24 and Mi-17 helicopters, Cessna 337 "Push and Pull" light bombers and anti-aircraft cannon emplacements flashed by our windows. I wondered which anti-aircraft emplacement shot down Smedley Müller and "Chepe" Robelo, the Miskito and Ladino ARDE pilots, when they flew out of the Caribbean sun on the first bombing attempt of Managua, 8 September 1983. Now some four and a half years later we were flying into Managua on the first negotiating attempt with the Sandinistas on their home ground.

We were stopped at the bottom of the stairs and told that we must go directly to greet Tomás Borge at his Ministry of Interior—the building that is bedecked with the Orwellian-like quotation "Sentinel of the Peoples' Happiness" and is the headquarters of the secret police, the prisons, the divine mobs, and the war against the Indian and Creole nations. Our delegation said no. We were not in Managua to make a kiss-the-ring visit to the headquarters of repression.

Sandinista State Security (DGSE) told us to stay where we were on the tarmac and the nearby Copa plane was ordered not to leave. After an hour the frustrated pilot swung the plane around and took off leaving us standing in the dark. State Security took us inside to the VIP lounge where we were kept while several "sí, mi Comandante" telephone calls were made. After two hours of this rigmarole, orders were given to take our passports and to detain us under armed

60

A detachment of Miskito and Creole fighters in southern Yapti Tasba, 1984.

guard at the hotel across from the airport until morning when
we would be expelled from Nicaragua on the first plane out.
Another round of negotiations with the Sandinistas had begun.

The wall and the club
A prisoner was taken by a guard to a stone wall and told
to hit his head against it. The prisoner refused and the guard
beat him on the head with a club until he complied with
the order. After a few self-inflicted blows, the prisoner stopped
and stood back from the wall. "Why are you stopping?" the
guard asked, "I didn't tell you how hard you must hit your
head. Keep going or I must hit you and I will hit you harder."
"No," said the prisoner, "I am more free when you hit me."

With international opinion favoring negotiations with the
Sandinistas and with Central America's largest army occu-
pying their nations, the Indian-Creole resistance faces the wall
and the club. Misurasata and Yatama have carried out seven
rounds of negotiations with the Sandinistas from 1984-1988.
And the Sandinistas have carried out seven years of war and
repression against the Miskito, Sumo, Rama and Creole (black)
peoples. The FSLN (Frente Sandinista de Liberación Nacional) used the negotiations to gain time and ground on the Indian-Creole military-political resistance forces while organiz-
ing smokeless weapons to strengthen their grip on the occupied nations.

To suppress resistance to their occupation, the Sandinistas
burned to the ground sixty-five Miskito and thirty Sumo
communities; forcibly displaced 70,000 Miskitos and Sumos
(one-half of the population) into state camps and external refugee camps; carried out arbitrary mass arrests, jailings and
torture; sent Soviet helicopter gunships and elite army and
security forces to attack Indian communities because they oppose the occupation; imposed hunger and food dependency
by destroying crops, fruit trees and fishing canoes, and restrict-

ing access to staples such as rice and beans; outlawed any independent Indian government or organizations and replaced them with an FSLN occupation government and Sandinista organizations; conscripted—often forcibly—Indian and Creole youths into the invader's army and security forces; and then used Soviet-style autonomy laws in an effort to stamp out the peoples' wishes for self-determination. Because none of these counterinsurgency tactics worked to quell the peoples' resistance to the occupation and demands for FSLN withdrawal from their territories, the Sandinistas decided to use the tactic of peace negotiations.

For the Sandinistas the negotiations were war by other means. Unable to establish firm control of the Indian and Creole territories by military means, the Frente Sandinista sought to use political "dialogue" to achieve four objectives: 1) stop the very effective Indian guerrilla resistance which was tying up and wearing down thousands of government army and security troops; 2) stop the civilian agitation for self-determination by incorporating the resistance leadership into the puppet government; 3) turn around the negative world opinion on Sandinista treatment of Indian peoples; and 4) guarantee an open back door to Cuba if the FDN (Fuerza Democrática Nicaragüense—the "contras") forced the FSLN from power and into the bush again. In 1984 the Sandinistas planned a double-track talk and shoot policy for the occupied territories to gain these objectives.

In 1984 the Indian and Creole resistance forces were divided between Misurasata (allied with Pastora's ARDE) and Misura (allied with Calero's and Bermúdez' FDN). The Boland Amendment had cut off U.S. overt military assistance to the anti-Sandinista groups and the subsequent covert deliveries were withheld from Misurasata and Misura by their Ladino "allies" who feared the Indians' autonomy goals. Though in ideological opposition, the left-wing ARDE and the right-wing FDN were in agreement over restricting weapons to a potent guerrilla force that might one day face them over the same question of control over the East Coast territories and resources. As a result, the only Indian army in the Americas had to fight Central America's largest army with few and small-caliber weapons. Instead of fielding as many as 15,000 fighters, Misurasata and Misura had a combined force of only 6,000 by late 1984 and most of them were low on or without ammunition, medicine, boots and often food, while the Sandinistas had a stranglehold on the Indian communities and began to receive sophisticated Soviet helicopter gunships and detection equipment to zero in on radio transmissions.

Running out of supplies, Misurasata agreed to negotiate with the FSLN beginning in December 1984. At worst Misurasata saw the negotiations as an opportunity for a time out in the war; at best the Misurasata leadership accepted that the Sandinistas were sincere about negotiating real solutions to the war. Misurasata entered negotiations seeking to end the Sandinista occupation. At the same time, the Sandinistas saw the negotiations as a way to strengthen their occupation.

During the 1984-85 negotiations and again in 1988 (as Yatama), Misurasata presented demands for: 1) withdrawal of FSLN military forces (EPS, MPS, FAS, DGSE, etc.) from the Indian and Creole nations, 2) withdrawal of Sandinista institutions (SMP, CDS, ENABAS, INPESCA, IRENA, ATC, CTS, MED, MINT, etc.), 3) retention of arms and formation of armed defense units in all Indian and Creole communities, 4) release of Indian and Creole people held in Sandinista prisons, 5) release of Indian and Creole people held in Sandinista "relocation" camps, 6) an investigation of Indian and Creole disappeared persons taken by Sandinista army and security forces, 7) recognition by the Nicaraguan state of the territorial (land and sea) boundaries of the Indian and Creole nations, 8) recognition by the Nicaraguan state that lands and resources within the demarcated Indian and Creole nations are inalienable, 9) rights to self-government and self-determination within the territorially autonomous nations, 10) indemnification for Sandinista-destroyed communities, stolen goods and confiscated property, 11) freedom to receive international reconstruction and development assistance, and 12) a formal bilateral peace treaty between the Nicaraguan government and Yapti Tasba (the collective name for the Indian and Creole nations).

Background to the negotiations

The Sandinistas did not change their overall no-concessions posture during the three and a half year life of the negotiations despite changing internal and external circumstances: military and economic setbacks occurred; some international political pressure was exerted; the negotiations were held in three different countries; the leadership of the FSLN delegation was changed, and finally brought under the supervision of the FSLN's national directorate; and the talks were conducted with and without mediation.

The negotiations took place during periods when the Sandinista military was weak and losing ground (1984-85) and during a period when it was strong and gaining ground (1988). Similarly, negotiations occurred when the Sandinista economy was barely showing gains and at other times when—in the words of Minister of Interior Tomás Borge—"it has crashed like 1929."

The other war affected the Sandinistas in negotiations with Misurasata and Yatama. The status of the contra-Sandinista war changed dramatically during the forty-one months that spanned the negotiations. The contras experienced military setbacks due to the Boland Amendment, negative Washington response on military assistance, revelations about Oliver North and "RIG," and the emergence of the gold brick Arias Peace Plan. And the contras experienced considerable military successes during periods when they received assistance from the

United States and other countries, especially the $100 million during 1986-87 when only $26 million was spent on the arms used to drive the Sandinistas out of much of the countryside and to the negotiating table at Sapoá.

International pressure was placed on the Sandinistas to negotiate in good faith and to resolve their war with the Indian nations. Guarantors and observers to the negotiations included ambassadors and representatives from Canada, France, West Germany, Holland, Denmark, Norway, Sweden, Cuba, Costa Rica, Colombia and Mexico; leaders of many indigenous nations and organizations such as Samiland (Nordic Sami Council), Newe Segobia (Western Shoshone National Council), Haudenosaunee (Six Nations Confederacy), the Inuit Circumpolar Conference (ICC), National Indian Youth Council (NIYC), Organización Nacional Indígena de Colombia, the American Indian Movement (AIM), and the World Council of Indigenous Peoples (WCIP).

The four 1984-1985 negotiations were carried out under the sponsorship of the governments of Colombia and Mexico. From 1985 to 1987, fighting resumed and intensified between the Sandinista occupation army and the Indian-Creole Resistance (Misurasata, Kisan, Misura—unified as Yatama in June 1987). In 1988 the negotiations began again and took place in Managua where they were mediated by the Conciliation Commission made up of representatives from the Moravian Church of Nicaragua, the Evangelical Committee for Development (CEPAD) and the U.S. Mennonite Central Committee.

In 1984-85 the Sandinista negotiation delegation was headed by Comandantes Luis Carrión and Omar Cabezas, both from the Ministry of Interior. The Sandinistas' 1988 delegation to the negotiations was headed by Minister of Interior Tomás Borge who reported daily to the FSLN's National Directorate. The Misurasata (1984-85) and Yatama (1988) delegations included Brooklyn Rivera, Armstrong Wiggins, Marcos

Hoppington, Modesto Watson, Samuel Mercado, Walter Ortiz, David Rodríguez, Marty Downs, Julian Smith, Herta Downs, Jenelee Hodgson and many others.

The negotiations

Agreement to negotiate came about through a secret October 1984 meeting between Senator Ted Kennedy, Daniel Ortega, and Misurasata coordinator Brooklyn Rivera in a New York City hotel room. As a precondition to formal negotiations, Ortega promised to release political prisoners (not done) and to permit a Misurasata delegation to visit the occupied Indian and Creole territories. The Misurasata delegation and accompanying foreign observers made a rousing eleven-day visit to the occupied nations. A prisoner exchange was made as a demonstration of good faith. Misurasata released three captive Sandinistas—Ray Hooker, Patricia Delgado, and Santiago Mayorga (who had been held for two months); the Sandinistas released Ariel Zúniga, Dennis Castro and Anastacio Forbes who had been in prison for three and a half years. As a precursor to formal negotiations, both sides agreed not to carry out any offensive military actions. However, on 31 October 1984, the day the Misurasata delegation departed Managua for Costa Rica, Sandinista Army and State Security attacked Haulover, a Miskito coastal community and a center of civilian support for Misurasata. Nearby Misurasata fighters rushed to defend Haulover. The Sandinistas suffered twenty-six dead, Misurasata two.

This occurrence of a Sandinista agreement and then attack foreshadowed other acts of political sabotage that were to take place during the negotiations. If there was an impending vote on contra aid in Washington, the Sandinistas would make concessions in the negotiations, publicize them, and then forget about them after the vote in Washington (23 April 1985 and 3 February 1988). If there was no impending vote in Washington, the Sandinistas would make no concessions, promote a signed promise to continue the negotiations, publicize that, and then launch attacks on Indian communities (January 1985, May 1985, February 1988).

As the negotiations progressed, it became clearly evident that the entire Sandinista strategy boiled down to getting a cease-fire by offering only promises to Misurasata-Yatama, and because that didn't work, to get a de facto cease-fire by using the negotiations as propaganda to cut off outside support to the Indian-Creole resistance organizations.

The first round: Bogotá, Colombia, 6-9 December 1984

President Belisario Betancur of Colombia, who had just negotiated a cease-fire with the M-19 insurgency, agreed to host and facilitate a meeting between the FSLN and Misurasata in late 1984. This was the first negotiation between an armed resistance force and a state government in any of Central America's wars.

The FSLN presented a one-item agenda: in exchange for a cease-fire, Misurasata fighters and exiles would receive amnesty. The FSLN rejected a nine-page treaty proposal submitted by Misurasata that called for a Sandinista pull-out from the occupied Indian and Creole nations.

It was evident that the Sandinistas did not come to Bogotá to negotiate—they had no position documents nor detailed proposals of their own; they came to get a cease-fire for which Comandante Luis Carrión could only offer some vague promises about working on Indian land rights "after the war is over."

But the Sandinistas had another agenda which they brought up at a long afternoon cocktail break when Comandante Omar Cabezas began talking about the security of the East Coast being necessary in case the Sandinistas had to to bail out of Managua. In December 1984 the FSLN was in a desperate predicament: their army was stretched to the limit fighting on three fronts (against the FDN in the north, ARDE in the

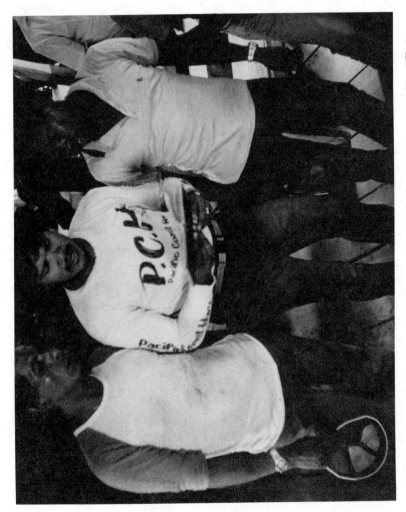

Misura and Misurasata military commanders at a church service in FSLN-occupied Yapti Tasba. Resistance forces guard community.

south, and Misurasata and Misura in the east). Some in the FSLN leadership saw that it was necessary to prepare alternatives if the Sandinistas were forced to abandon the government and again become guerrillas. But this time not one of the countries that border Nicaragua would harbor FSLN guerrillas. Instead, the Sandinistas would have to concentrate their surviving forces inside Nicaragua in a region that was accessible to Cuba for supplies. But the Indian and Creole resistance controlled the coast and rivers and could prevent any future sea-river transport of arms from Cuba to FSLN guerrillas in the mountains. This is also what they had come to Bogotá to talk about but not in the negotiation sessions. Brooklyn Rivera responded that Misurasata wanted to end one war, not lay plans for another.

Omar Cabezas said, "Quit fighting us. Join our revolution. Work with us. We promise to resolve your problems when the war is over. We will need each other in the future."

Armstrong Wiggins, Misurasata's ambassador at large, told Omar Cabezas and the rest of the Sandinista delegation, "We will never join you. We will never become Sandinista. Your ship is sinking and you want us to get on board with you. This we won't do. We will negotiate a cease-fire in exchange for a withdrawal from our land and we will negotiate a bilateral relationship with you. But first your government has to recognize that the land and resources are ours. We want territorial autonomy, not Sandinista promises."

With no movement on the issue of recognition of Indian land and resource rights, the negotiations became deadlocked. Agreement was reached to meet again in January. After one round of negotiations, no gains had been made in ending the Sandinista war against the Indian nations.

Misurasata's proposal promoted territorial autonomy as the key to ending the war between the Sandinista state and the Indian and Creole nations. The FSLN delegation would not consider any discussions with Misurasata over autonomy. At the same time, December 1984, the FSLN launched its own autonomy project for "the Atlantic Coast of Nicaragua" and created a Sandinista Autonomy Commission headed by Minister of Interior Tomás Borge.

In late December 1984, Brooklyn Rivera and other exiled Misurasata leaders went by sea from Costa Rica to the occupied Indian nations. They went to tell the people about the stalemated outcome of the December negotiations and to obtain their opinions for the next round, which was scheduled for 19-20 January.

On 1 January 1985 the Sandinistas began a widespread, coordinated air and ground assault against Miskito communities along 100 miles of coastline between Puerto Cabezas and Bluefields. An EPS (Ejército Popular Sandinista) force sent from Bluefields to the Pearl Lagoon area was guided by Santiago Mayorga, a member of Sandinista State Security (DGSE) who had been a prisoner held by Misurasata and released in the October 1984 Misurasata-FSLN prisoner exchange. Sandinista Air Force bombing, rockets and machine gun strafing of Miskito villages were done in coordination with EPS ground assaults. Civilian communities suffered scattered bombing and rocket strikes and then EPS and DGSE beatings, arrests and occupations in Kara, Little Sandy Bay, Río Grande Bar, Wounta and Haulover. Several sources from Puerto Cabezas reported artillery fire from that city's Lamlaya river landing directed toward the nearby Miskito community of Karata (Misurasata leader Armstrong Wiggins' home town). During the combined EPS-DGSE ground and FAS (Fuerza Aérea Sandinista) air attack on Río Grande Bar, Brooklyn Rivera and Britanico Cutberth were wounded by rocket shrapnel.

Under heavy siege, the Misurasata leadership managed to evacuate Río Grande Bar by sea and headed for Costa Rica pursued by a Sandinista patrol vessel. Alerted by radio, an armed Misurasata *dori* (sea-going dugout canoe) arrived in

71

time to drive off the Sandinista vessel. In Costa Rica, Britanico Cutberth's foot had to be amputated.

Misurasata informed the Sandinistas and Colombia's President Belisario Betancur that it was breaking off negotiations because of the continuing bombings and military occupation of Miskito communities.

The negotiations resumed due to the personal intervention of President Betancur. During the 1 March 1985 inauguration of Uruguay's President Julio Sanguinetti, President Betancur met with Daniel Ortega to ask him to pull back the Sandinista military so that the talks could continue. Then on 10 March President Betancur met secretly with Brooklyn Rivera on the island of San Andrés to ask him to continue the talks in late March.

The second round: Bogotá, Colombia, 26-27 March 1985
Again the Sandinistas rejected Misurasata's treaty proposal to end their occupation of the East Coast territories. At the same time, the Sandinistas countered with another offer of amnesty in exchange for a cease-fire.

The Sandinistas claimed absolute sovereignty over Indian nations, peoples and resources. Misurasata's demands for self-government, self-determination and self-defense were interpreted by the FSLN delegation as "threats to Nicaraguan sovereignty."

Underlying all of the negotiations was the still unsettled dispute of sovereignty over the Indian and Creole territories. As the Nicaraguan government, the Sandinistas claimed sovereignty over the East Coast but could produce no historical or contemporary bill of sale or any other verification of how they actually got rights to Indian peoples' countries. The Miskito, Sumo and Rama peoples have never lost or given away their sovereignty, territory or rights of self-determination. For 500 years the Miskito, especially, had resisted, militarily and politically, attempted invasions and occupations of their country. For the last century, the Nicaraguans had tried to annex the East Coast nations by demographic, political and economic osmosis: unfettered migration; Siberia-like exile of politicians, doctors, educators and soldiers to colonize the territories for Mother Nicaragua; and Brooklyn Bridge leases to foreign companies to exploit Indian lumber and gold. When the Sandinistas took over in 1979 they decided to accelerate the process of creeping annexation by simply decreeing that Indian and Creole peoples were exploited Nicaraguan minorities, and that as the vanguard of the Nicaraguan people, the FSLN would insure the end of such exploitation by expropriating all of the Indian and Creole territories, a collective area larger and richer than Costa Rica.

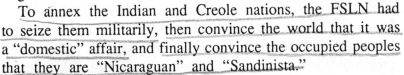

To annex the Indian and Creole nations, the FSLN had to seize them militarily, then convince the world that it was a "domestic" affair, and finally convince the occupied peoples that they are "Nicaraguan" and "Sandinista."

The propaganda the FSLN pumped out to cover up their occupation and the territorial base of the war is that the Indian and Creole peoples are but an ethnic minority of the Nicaraguan population who are duped by Washington's agents into claiming historically distinct identities and territories in order to separate one-half of Nicaragua and turn it over to the "imperialists." Imagine a similar assertion by the Nazis if they had claimed that the French are but a German ethnic group manipulated by British agents into believing they are a distinct people and that western Germany is really France.

At the huge mahogany negotiation table in the ornate Palacio de San Carlos in Bogotá, sat representatives of two revolutions: one side of the table said they were the future of Latin America and that the Indians could survive only as ethnic groups; the other side of the table said they were the future of Indian America and that the Ladino Revolution had no place on Indian land.

Sandinista Comandante Luis Carrión said that "the Nicaraguan government is disposed to making special considerations to protect the culture of Indians as Nicaraguan ethnic groups." To this Misurasata coordinator Brooklyn Rivera responded: "Ethnic groups run restaurants. We have an army. We are a people. We want self-determination."

Increasingly uncomfortable in being challenged over sovereignty, the Sandinista delegation could do no more than make a boldface declaration that the armed conflict was a "domestic issue," an internal dispute between Nicaraguans subject to no international scrutiny, monitoring, arbitration or mediation.

But Misurasata had invited representatives of twenty indigenous nations and organizations to the negotiations and they kept the issue of sovereignty very much alive. The Sandinistas became very agitated over the presence of Indian observers at the negotiations who represented the American Indian Movement, Haudenosaunee—Six Nations Confederacy, National Indian Youth Council, World Council of Indigenous Peoples, Organización Nacional Indígena de Colombia, Western Shoshone Nation, Asociación Interétnica para el Desarrollo de la Selva Peruana and many other indigenous nations and organizations.

Comandante Luis Carrión said that these Indian observers at the negotiations "are a threat to the sovereignty of Nicaragua." To this Chief Oren Lyons from the Six Nations Confederacy responded that "it is the Sandinista position that is a threat to the Indians," and Russell Means (AIM) remarked, "the Sandinistas say that we are a threat to their sovereignty; we have to carve that one in granite."

John Mohawk (Six Nations Confederacy), who as former editor of *Akwesasne Notes* had followed the war from the start, pointed out during a coffee break with the Sandinista delegation: "You Nicaraguans go through all sorts of gyrations to hide the facts that your people have invaded the coast, and that you look different, talk different, are in a different

74

place—not your home, and are there with guns. I call this imperialism. What do you call it?"

Clutching his throat, Sandinista Comandante Omar Cabezas turned to the Misurasata delegation, "We've had it up to here with you Indians." Misurasata's Armstrong Wiggins asked him if he was accusing the Indians of creating the problem.

After two rounds of negotiations, no gains had been made toward ending the Sandinista war against the Indian nations.

The third round: Mexico City, Mexico, 20-22 April 1985

The day before a U.S. vote on contra aid the FSLN signed a 22 April agreement that they would lift their military blockade of Indian villages, distribute desperately needed food and medicine, allow freedom of movement for villagers to fish, hunt and plant, and release Indian and Creole prisoners (something Daniel Ortega had promised to do in October 1984). In return, Misurasata agreed to another round of negotiations. The Sandinistas and Misurasata made an agreement to stop offensive military actions. Managua immediately called the no-escalation agreement a cease-fire and rushed the news to their supporters in Washington. The Sandinistas were only interested in influencing the contra aid vote; they did not allow any shipments of food and medicine to reach the villages, nor were the villagers permitted to hunt, fish or plant.

On 25 April Minister of Interior Tomás Borge went to the occupied nations to assert: "Here there are no whites, blacks, Miskitos or Creoles. Here there are revolutionary and counterrevolutionary Nicaraguans, regardless of the color of their skin. The only thing that differentiates us is the attitude we assume toward the nation" (*New York Times,* 26 April 1985, p. 6).

On 28 April 1985 the Sandinistas released fourteen Miskito prisoners from jail in Puerto Cabezas.

In late April and May, Sandinista State Security units pos-

ing as Red Cross workers went into Miskito villages to ask
for the locations of the Misurasata fighters so that the "Red
Cross" could deliver "the medicine." On 9 May the lower
Río Grande (Awaltara) region was attacked by EPS units and
Kara was again bombed. Misurasata set ambushes against
EPS troop movements on the Alamikamba-Limbaika road.
Fighting broke out again around and in several Miskito
communities. On 17 May a Misurasata unit headed by
Comandantes Coyote and Danto attacked the Sandinista gar-
rison in Bluefields. Many Creole people in the Sandinista Mi-
litia (MPS) turned their weapons against the Sandinista Army
(EPS). The Sandinista Army killed twenty-six MPS and
Misurasata people, loaded the bodies into a dump truck, drove
to the city's central park, and dumped them into a pile where
they were left as a warning for two days. Families were for-
bidden to retrieve the bodies.

The fourth round: Bogotá, Colombia, 25-26 May 1985
The Sandinistas presented Misurasata a list of supposed
"cease-fire violations" (kidnappings, assassinations, destruction of state property and so on) and then made hard-line
demands to Misurasata that it must sign a cease-fire or face
the military consequences. Misurasata again presented its
proposals for a Sandinista military and institutional pull out
from Indian and Creole territory (which would end the war)
and the establishment of Indian and Creole local government
and defense forces. The Sandinistas categorically rejected these
and all the other Misurasata proposals. As a result the talks
collapsed.

Comandante Luis Carrión, head of the Sandinista negotiation
delegation, said, "This proposal is completely beyond any
political or military reality. Besides being politically unacceptable because it would limit Government authority over
national territory, militarily it would give away every advantage to the groups fighting there" (the *New York Times*, 30

76

Returning body of a civilian killed in fight between FSLN-EPS occupation troops and Indian resistance fighters.

May, p. 3). (Actually there would be no more fighting if the Sandinistas left the occupied nations.)

After four rounds no gains had been made in ending the Sandinista war against the Indian nations. In May 1985 Minister of Interior Tomás Borge reorganized Sandinista control of the Indian and Creole nations and placed himself as government head of all the occupied nations. Only the Indian and Creole nations have such centralized FSLN control.

Borge became Nicaragua's "second president." Not only was he FSLN head of a vast occupied territory, he controlled the entire repressive apparatus: State Security, the prisons, the CDS informers and vigilantes, the "divine mobs," a personal 5000-man Ministry of Interior special forces army, access to food and medicine, and the FSLN's Autonomy Commission.

Resistance leader Modesto Watson accused Tomás Borge of being a "modern William Walker." "Borge is in *our* country today just like William Walker was in *their* country last century. In our nations Borge is a foreigner, he doesn't speak the language, he doesn't know the culture or history, he doesn't respect the people, he wasn't invited to come, he is only there by force of arms, and the people don't want him. He is Tomás Walker."

The Sandinistas suspended contact with Misurasata. The negotiations appeared to be over for good. Tomás Borge pushed his State Security people to make contact with Indian commanders of Misurasata and Misura units to offer personal ceasefires. At this time, the North American Congress's Boland Amendment had prevented resupply of all anti-Sandinista groups including the FDN and ARDE and indirectly Misura and Misurasata. All of the fighters were desperately low on ammunition, medicine and boots.

Misura's Comandante Eduardo Pantin and his men were the first to sign a cease-fire with the Sandinistas. This formed the core of what came to be "Kisan Por La Paz," a collection of Indian combat units that kept their weapons, had freedom of movement between Puerto Cabezas and the village of Yulu, received food and some money from the FSLN, and were frequently visited by the media.

The fifth round: Managua, Nicaragua, 25 January-2 February, 1988

On 7 August 1987 the presidents of five Central American states signed the Esquipulas II agreement. These accords are concerned with only three of the nine wars in Central America —the insurgencies that seek to overthrow state governments in Guatemala, El Salvador and Nicaragua. The other six wars against indigenous nations in Central America are not included. Esquipulas II (the Arias Peace Plan) is a plan for incumbent state governments. This initiative set in motion political forces that brought the FSLN and the RN (Resistencia Nicaragüense, formerly the FDN) to the negotiation table in March 1988. Esquipulas II did not lead to the reopening of negotiations with the Miskito-Creole resistance now united as Yatama.

On 7 September 1987 President Daniel Ortega signed into Nicaraguan law the FSLN's Autonomy Statute to camouflage the Sandinista occupation of the Yapti Tasba nations.

Despite the FSLN's proclamations that the East Coast was now autonomous, that the Indian fighters had signed cease-fires, that peace was at hand, and that the Indian and Creole people supported the Managua government, the situation in the occupied nations had actually changed very little. The people detest the Sandinistas, who will never be forgiven for burning down the villages and for the forced relocations. With good military equipment from the $5 million appropriated by the U.S. Congress, the Yatama forces effectively engaged some of the best Sandinista units, including regular EPS and special anti-guerrilla "BLI" and "Cazador" forces. For the first time Indian forces had weapons equivalent to that of their enemies and from August 1987 the fighting intensified in the Miskito nation.

In September the Sandinistas began to send signals that they would like to reopen negotiations. Tomás Borge called Brooklyn Rivera in Costa Rica and engaged in several hours of late night conversation. Negotiations were to begin in October but the FSLN imposed impossible demands on Yatama, including the provision that the Yatama leaders accept FSLN amnesty, travel to Managua without assurances of safety or valid visas and passports, and agree to a list of preconditions. Yatama leaders said they would not accept amnesty because they had done nothing wrong except to defend their nations against the Sandinista invasion and aggression. The planned October talks were off.

In January 1988, Daniel Ortega and other Central American presidents came to San José, Costa Rica for a summit to discuss Esquipulas II, the peace plan agreed to in Guatemala, 7 August 1987. Brooklyn Rivera and Samuel Mercado met with Ortega at this time and it was agreed to reopen negotiations in Managua at the end of January. No preconditions would be demanded of Yatama. And Yatama would be allowed to visit Puerto Cabezas and Bluefields.

Upon arrival in Managua on Saturday, 23 January the Yatama negotiation delegation was ordered to go to the Ministry of Interior to be received by Tomás Borge, who was to head the FSLN's negotiation team. Yatama refused because the Ministry of Interior occupies and represses the Indian nations (DGSE, MINT special forces, CDS, the prison system, and the FSLN's Autonomy Commission). The delegation was held by State Security at the airport for three hours and then taken by DGSE and MINT soldiers to the Hotel Las Mercedes with orders to be deported the next morning. Surrounded by news reporters asking where the delegation was, Tomás Borge relented and phoned the delegation to suggest another meeting place.

Instead of holding them under house arrest at the hotel, Comandante Borge invited the Yatama delegation to his restaurant, Mirador, with its charming location overlooking Lago Tiscapa, where Somoza agents used to dispose of the bodies of dissidents, and just down the street from El Chipote, the FSLN's loathsome maximum security prison which is under Borge's personal direction.

Borge is a one-half scale version of Castro, minus the beard but complete with cigar, unadorned military clothes, capricious decisions, and long-winded monologues. Framed in cigar smoke he rambled on to Rivera for two hours with the Sandinista version of Miskito history: the Miskito are an ethnic group created by British and American colonialists and kept marginalized from assimilating as Nicaraguans in order to exploit Miskito labor and the coast's resources. Borge believes the propaganda that his own Ministry shovels out!

Meanwhile a State Security photographer took pictures of each of the Yatama delegation and advisors while two Ministry of Interior bodyguards with briefcases hovered nearby.

Afterwards, Borge leaned back and said to Rivera, " I don't know about you but when I am in situations like this I like to have a weapon. We'll give you some so you can protect yourself on the coast."

Rivera responded, "But we have your guarantee of safe conduct, so your soldiers won't shoot us. The only other people with weapons on the coast are our fighters and they won't shoot at us, their leaders, so we don't need any weapons." (Despite this refusal, three days later Soviet revolvers, ammunition, extra clips and holsters were delivered and Yatama immediately returned them to the Ministry of Interior delivery man.)

"Well, we don't have much more to offer you than weapons—we have a lot of those. Do you need money? We have a lot of that, too. It is not worth much but you can have all you want." Borge was working down his compromise list.

"No thank you."

The next day, Sunday, 24 January, Yatama received a hand-delivered letter, signed in e.e. cummings-style all lower case by Tomás Borge confirming that the negotiations would be "bilateral," "at the highest level," and "without conditions."

But on Monday, only a minor official showed up to head the Sandinista delegation, Mirna Cunningham, a Miskito. Yatama sent word that since the conflict was not between Miskito people there was nothing to negotiate with Miskito people. Instead of going to the negotiations, Yatama people met opposition people in labor, the Catholic church and *La Prensa* newspaper. That provoked a response and the next day Borge and his advisors, José "Chepe" González and Salvador Pérez, arrived to begin negotiating.

The Sandinistas opened with a demand that Yatama's "gringo" advisors "abandon the country" immediately as these negotiations were a "domestic" matter. Yatama said that the FSLN uses gringo advisors all the time, and that the issue on the table was self-determination for Indian peoples, and therefore Yatama, not the Sandinistas, would determine who would be their advisors. Besides, not all the advisors were gringos. Borge took the matter to the FSLN's National Directorate and came back with a compromise: the non-Indian advisors—Bernard Nietschmann and Steve Tullberg—would have to leave, the others—Jim Anaya and Glenn Morris—could stay. Yatama's reply was no. Everybody stays.

Later when the negotiations resumed, Borge confided a "my grandmother was Cherokee princess" story to the Yatama delegation: "One of my ancestors may have been Indian. My grandmother. She was probably Miskito. I'm having this investigated right now. If this is true, I have Miskito blood in me. That's probably why I feel so close to the Indian people on the coast."

On 2 February, one day before a vote on contra aid in the United States House of Representatives, the FSLN signed a preliminary accord agreeing to fifteen of Yatama's thirty-two proposed steps to end the war, including a conditional cease-fire for the duration of the negotiations. The FSLN rushed news of the accord to their representatives in Washington. Several swing-vote congressmen who are supportive of Indian rights in Nicaragua voted against military assistance to the contras and the assistance package narrowly lost.

As they had in April 1985, the FSLN timed the negotiations and some paper concessions to block Washington's military assistance to the armed resistance. And again, once the vote was over, the Sandinistas kept none of their agreements —not one of the fifteen.

After five rounds of negotiations no gains had been made in ending the Sandinista war against the Indian nations.

The sixth round: Managua, Nicaragua, 29 February-16 March 1988

Yatama made this round conditional upon the Sandinistas allowing the delegation to visit the occupied Indian nations. The FSLN stopped the delegation from going to the Sumu nation because of supposed fighting and ordered Yatama to go first to Bluefields "to avoid being shot down by a contra missile" enroute from Managua to Puerto Cabezas. Yatama advisor Clem Chartier (previous president of the World Council of Indigenous Peoples) asked the Sandinistas: "Is the red eye flight cheaper?"

In Managua, permission had been given to Yatama to use the radio and to hold a night meeting in Bluefields, but when the delegation arrived, State Security turned off the city's electricity. The Moravian church had a generator and the meeting was held in their gymnasium.

Meanwhile, the Sandinistas threatened the people in every

community on Yatama's itinerary. The DGSE told the people of Yulu and the Kisan Por La Paz cease-fire group that they would not receive their food supplies unless they threw stones at the Yatama delegation. In Puerto Cabezas, Sandinista Governor Mirna Cunningham spoke on the Voz Popular del Pueblo radio and said that food and permission to receive medicine and doctor's care would be cut off to those who went to meet with or listen to the delegation. Then, on 12 March Ladino *turbas* imported from Managua used stones, lead pipes, and 2x4's to attack the hotel where the Yatama delegation was staying in Puerto Cabezas. Miskito people drove off the *turbas*. That night in a continuing effort to intimidate the Miskito people in Puerto Cabezas and the delegation, Sandinista Army and Security people fired machine guns just over the hotel's roof top and artillery rounds were fired from close by.

On Sunday, 13 March, in order to stop people from going to the baseball stadium to listen to the delegation, the Sandinistas cordoned off Puerto Cabezas, shot off antiaircraft cannons and heavy-caliber machine guns just outside the stadium, and then unleashed their *turba* goons (Borge's "divine mobs") who tried to attack the delegation with rocks, pipes, baseball bats, 2x4's and pistols. Three people in the Conciliation Commission (mediators in the negotiations) were wounded by the *turbas* before the Miskito audience rose up to defend the Commission and the Yatama delegation.

When the negotiations resumed in Managua on 14 March the Sandinista delegation rejected Yatama's proposals to reach agreements on Indian self-government, self-determination, self-defense and demarcation of the Yapti Tasba Indian and Creole nations. The Sandinistas wanted a cease-fire and Yatama wanted a cease-occupation.

After six rounds of negotiations, no gains had been made in ending the Sandinista war against the Indian nations.

Bruno Gabriel (upraised arm), head military commander, killed during a 2000-man FSLN/EPS attack ten days after this picture was taken.

The seventh round: Managua, Nicaragua, 9-14 May 1988
During these talks, the Sandinista delegation took their hardest stance yet, swept aside the 2 February Preliminary Accords; demanded that Yatama agree to a cease-fire, accept FSLN amnesty, and integrate themselves into the FSLN's Soviet-style "autonomy process"; prohibited the Yatama delegation from again visiting the occupied Indian nations; and charged that the government could not accept any points in the Yatama peace proposal because all were "unconstitutional."

Tomás Borge, head of the FSLN's negotiating team, told the Yatama delegation, "When we were fighting in the mountains we *never* considered negotiating with Somoza. We fought to overthrow his government. You call yourselves revolutionaries. Why are you here negotiating?"

The talks collapsed after the peace proposal presented by Yatama was rejected by the FSLN as being "unacceptable from the military, political and legal point of view." In a press conference, Sub-Comandante José González, head of the Sandinista occupation and one of the FSLN's chief negotiators, said that Yatama's demand for a pull out of the Sandinista Armed Forces from Indian communities was "absurd." Furthermore, Sub-Comandante González said that Yatama's proposal for autonomy based on indigenous territory would "exacerbate ethnic differentiation and would signify the retreat of peace," and that to claim a separate territory was "racist" and "ethnocentric" (*Nuevo Diario*, 15 May 1988, pp. 1, 8). According to the Sandinistas, Indian people would not be "racist" or "ethnocentric" if they gave up their nations and territory to the Sandinista state.

Nicaraguan President Daniel Ortega was quoted in the *New York Times* (22 May 1988) as justifying the end of the negotiations with Yatama because "Rivera does not represent anyone. He came to ask that the government recognize and legalize the independence of the Atlantic Coast. This is totally absurd."

Nicaraguan Ambassador to the United States, Carlos Tunnermann wrote in a letter to the *New York Times* (9 June 1988), "The Miskito Indian rebels with whom the Government has been negotiating are seeking Indian control over nearly a third of Nicaragua....the demands of a minority of leaders approach outright separatism which no sovereign government could responsibly accommodate." In other words, the Sandinistas were not going to negotiate nor relinquish their occupation of the Indian nations, seizure of Indian resources, and imposition of Sandinista repressive institutions and organizations.

Nothing gained and a lot lost
After participating in negotiations that began in 1984 Yatama learned that the Sandinista government never had any intention of making concessions on Indian rights that would end their war against the Indian peoples and their repressive occupation of the Indian and Creole nations. Instead, the Sandinistas have used the negotiations as propaganda to cut off outside military assistance to the Indian and Creole fighters, to promote a false international image of conciliation, and to strengthen their military and institutional grip on the occupied nations. The Sandinistas are unwilling to cease their occupation of the Indian-Creole nations and to permit Indian and Creole self-government and self-determination over Indian and Creole lands, waters and resources. Liberty, freedom and democracy will not come from negotiations with the Sandinistas.

Negotiations with the Sandinistas are fruitless without major military pressure on the Sandinistas. Negotiations with the Sandinistas are fruitless without serious political pressure on the Sandinistas from their Central American neighbors and the international community. As it stands now there is no military or political pressure on the Sandinistas.

President Oscar Arias of Costa Rica promised that when

87

the fighting was over he and other Central American presidents would exert strong political pressure on the Sandinistas to force democratic reforms. President Arias did not keep his promise.

The negotiations with Misurasata-Yatama gave the Sandinistas breathing room to survive and entrench in the occupied nations. The Sandinistas forced their nonnegotiable brand of autonomy on the occupied nations, they signed cease-fires with supply-short Indian resistance commanders, and they produced propaganda for international consumption that the war with the Indians was over.

Peace without liberty

But the war is not over. The reasons for the war persist: occupation, oppression, conscription, exploitation, expropriation. There are only two ways to be on Indian land: by invitation or by invasion. And the Sandinista invaders are not going home. They are nailing down their occupation with permanent military bases, a puppet government, indoctrination in their schools, forced participation in their mass organizations, and total control of food and work. The Sandinista occupation grinds the people down, day after day, into deeper misery, poverty and dependency.

Peace has been declared by the FSLN in the occupied territories: peace without liberty, peace without freedom, peace without basic rights, peace without food, peace without work. Peace is hell.

To maintain Sandinista-style peace, the FSLN must themselves continue the war. Even though there is now no fighting the Sandinistas must assert that war is imminent to justify their continuing militarization of the occupied nations. Even though there is no outside military assistance to Yatama, the FSLN must maintain the specter of "imperialist-backed aggression" to justify their continuing denial of Indian and Creole demands for territorial and resource rights, self-government and self-determination in what are now occupied nations. Even though they have proclaimed autonomy, the Sandinista invaders must maintain rigid military control of the occupied nations because they don't trust the Miskito, Sumo, Rama and Creole peoples including those they've installed in their occupation government and those with whom they've signed cease-fires.

It is likely that the war will begin again. It is extremely unlikely that negotiations between Yatama and the FSLN will begin again. The cease-fires that Borge engineered and then parlayed into his pet project, "Kisan Por La Paz," have come unraveled because no FSLN promises were kept, no land rights granted, and no autonomy was possible. On 9 September, 2000 Indian fighters—almost everyone who had signed cease-fires—renounced the hollow agreements that produced nothing over three years and began again to prepare for war.

The economics of military occupation means that the Sandinistas and their allies must spend much more to impose their presence than the resistance does to oppose their presence. When the Sandinistas declared peace they lost the justification for outside military assistance so they may have to soon pay a larger share of the costs for their military occupation of the Yapti Tasba nations. At the same time, Yatama has reorganized to survive and resist even if no outside support is forthcoming.

U.S. Policy and Strategy for Nicaragua and Central America

OF THE WORLD'S most volatile geopolitical hot spots, Central America is the one closest to the United States and the only one with a landbridge connection to the United States. What happens in Central America is of extreme importance to the United States in terms of national security, regional security, refugees and as an example of American resolve and prestige.

Central America has proven to be a very difficult area for U.S. foreign policy. We have not seen the progress there that we have elsewhere with U.S. foreign policy, such as in Southwest Asia, Southeast Asia, Africa and the Soviet Union. Instead, the U.S. has experienced a number of exasperating setbacks in the very region where historically it has exercised the greatest economic and political influence. As of early 1989, Noriega remains in power in Panama as does the Soviet-and Cuban-backed Sandinista regime in Nicaragua, opposition to American presence grows in Honduras, the democratic gains in El Salvador and Guatemala are being eroded, and Costa Rica's President Arias pulled the rug out from under U.S. Nicaragua policy with his Esquipulas II peace plan.

Numerous persistent crises contribute to Central America's

escalating problems: insurgencies, totalitarian governments, Soviet and Cuban agendas, rising populations and declining economies, drug trafficking, destructive use of land and resources, hot-war refugees and widespread human rights violations. Many of these individual crises are interrelated and form tight clusters of political-economic problems of varying intensities and histories in different countries. This has three important consequences for any new U.S. policy toward Central America: 1) a flexible, multifaceted program is needed instead of a single uniform one, 2) most problems do not lend themselves to short-term solutions; this necessitates the development of clear, long-term objectives backed by a strong commitment that will endure, and 3) positive results in a couple of key countries will have a multiplier effect throughout the region.

Recent United States policy in the region has focused on three countries: Mexico because it is big, poor and next door; Panama because it has the canal; and Nicaragua because it has an oppressive and aggressive Marxist-Leninist regime. The strategic significance of Sandinista Nicaragua increased several fold on 10 February 1989 when the Sandinistas announced that Japan heads an investment group interested in financing an inter-oceanic canal across Nicaragua. Although a Nicaraguan canal has been an unrealized dream for more than 150 years, the possibility of a Sandinista-controlled modern canal, wide enough to permit passage of the largest ships, would give Nicaragua the hemisphere's most important economic and military chokepoint.

Unremitting and unavoidable Nicaragua

Nicaragua is the most important and most complicated foreign issue in Central America. Nicaragua is the source of many regional security problems because it is a base for Soviet and Cuban activities and strategies for Central America and because the Sandinistas themselves remain committed to supporting Communist insurgencies in neighboring countries. At the same time, the FSLN (Frente Sandinista de Liberación Nacional) has such a totalitarian chokehold on the country that it is an internal cancer, and suffering and misery increase daily and force people to vote with their feet and flee to other countries at the rate of one out of every five Nicaraguans to date, with more on the way. This increases political and economic burdens elsewhere in the region and the United States (particularly Brownsville and Miami) and reduces them in Nicaragua. To cover up the political embarrassment of such a massive outpouring of people from Nicaragua, the Sandinistas blame the exodus on U.S. imperialism and Hurricane "Joan" that slammed into the Southeast Coast, 22 October 1988.

In the face of these four factors—the Soviet-Cuban beachhead, the Sandinista threat to the region, the Sandinista repression against the Nicaraguan people, and the possibility of a Sandinista-controlled modern inter-oceanic canal—the U.S. must maintain its long-standing commitment and policy objectives to change the Nicaraguan regime. Failure to do so would be interpreted as a major foreign policy setback for the U.S. in its own backyard and an open-door signal throughout Latin America and elsewhere that Washington and the American people lack the resolve to confront Soviet-supported repressive regimes even within the Western Hemisphere.

Mirror, mirror on the wall
The questions of what should be our policy and strategy toward Sandinista Nicaragua and other countries in the Central American region will attract many suggestions and proposed programs during the period in which the Bush administration prepares new policies and overhauls existing ones. Many things are at a standstill in the region as leaders, governments, and movements await the outcome of these expected deliberations.

Consideration of a range of possible regional policies, objectives and strategies offered by current administration people, Central American specialists and Central American leaders will provide a full-deck, face up on the table perspective for the new administration. (Other possibilities will gradually emerge.)

One such policy statement now being circulated, authored by Richard N. Haass and titled "Major Alternative Scenarios For Nicaragua: Successful Negotiations," is a useful proving-ground forum for the negotiation perspective. Mr. Haass argues that democratization of Nicaragua can be produced through "successful negotiations" between the economically strapped Sandinistas, the economically orphaned contras, the United States and Central American countries. He envisions various scenarios leading to the negotiating table which produce an agreement for political pluralism and democracy, Sandinista regional nonintervention promises, and Soviet cutbacks or pullouts. All groups and interests give up something to get something.

Mr. Haass' paper represents "academic-blackboarding," where squares and circles and arrows are chalked in different combinations without recourse to a reality check, and the interests and agendas of each "actor" are assumed to be known, negotiable and rational. On Mr. Haass' two-dimensional blackboard, all interests become partial winners: the FSLN democratizes, the Resistencia Nicaragüense politically integrates, Latin American countries "rejoice," and the United States takes a bow for getting the contras politically inside Nicaragua and the Soviets and Cubans out of Nicaragua. While Mr. Haass' goals are laudable, his analysis rests on very precarious assumptions.

Mr. Haass' negotiation scenarios are based on the assumptions that the contras are "finished," that "the Sandinistas are likely to remain in power," that the greatest threat to the Sandinista revolution is "the marketplace," that the Sandinistas "might conclude they could institute a good deal of democracy and still prevail," that "for the Nicaraguan armed forces, any accord should be welcome," and that the Sandinistas and the Nicaraguan armed forces would trade "their current primacy and virtual assurance of continued domination for the uncertainties of political pluralism and the political marketplace."

Underlying these assumptions is the main premise that the Sandinistas would negotiate their revolution. Furthermore, Mr. Haass mistakenly characterizes the Sandinistas as being simply a political regime, albeit repressive, and that the Nicaraguan armed forces are somehow distinct.

Sandinista Nicaragua

The FSLN is the state and the state is the FSLN. The Sandinistas are not merely a government, they see themselves as an enduring, unchangeable vanguard that will eventually forge everything in Nicaragua into a concrete expression of their ideological beliefs.

The fact is that there can be no democracy, no liberty, no freedom, no political pluralism and no political marketplace in Nicaragua until the tentacles of the Sandinista regime can be forced to give up their stranglehold on Nicaragua and the Nicaraguan people.

In the Nicaraguan tropical forest there is a parasitic plant called the "strangler fig" which attaches itself to a tree for support and then grows by encircling the trunk and drawing nutrients until it literally squeezes the tree to death and replaces it as a viable and sustainable structure. Then the strangler fig reaches out to other nearby trees. The FSLN is like the strangler fig: it grows by squeezing the life out of Nicaragua until it becomes Nicaragua.

The FSLN is the army (EPS), the air force (FAS), the militia (MPS), and state security (DGSE); it is the economy (ENABAS) and the educational system (MED); and it is labor (CTS, ATC), women (AMNLAE), youth (JS 19), resources

95

(IRENA) and land (INRA). The FSLN exists and grows because it controls the lifeblood of most families: food and employment. And the FSLN maintains absolute control over dissent through its Ministry of Interior—the entrance of which is bedecked with the Orwellian phrase, "Sentinel of the Peoples' Happiness"—which administers the prisons, state security (DGSE), censors, neighborhood vigilantes (CDS), informants (*orejas*), and the paramilitary divine mob *(turbas)* and black beret *(boinas negras)* goon squads.

That is the FSLN. And that has to be dismantled to allow Nicaragua to determine democratically the nature and composition of a representative government. Those who believe that this can be done mainly through negotiations have not looked at the Sandinistas' track record on negotiations and have not listened to what the Sandinistas themselves say about negotiations.

Negotiating with the Sandinistas

Negotiations between opposed forces may occur for several reasons. Negotiations may be conducted to avert or prolong war, to end a stalemate, to extract concessions from a weakened adversary, to carry on a "smokeless" phase of conflict (war by other means), to stall for time to regroup, to gain world opinion leverage, and to go through the motions to silence domestic and international critics by demonstrating the intransigence of one's adversary.

All of these negotiation objectives pertain to talks that have and might be held with the Sandinistas.

The Sandinistas' track record in previous negotiations provides some insights into their likely behavior in any future negotiations. To date, the Sandinistas have held four rounds of negotiations with the RN (Resistencia Nicaragüense) and seven rounds with Misurasata-Yatama, the armed indigenous resistance that was the first to take up arms against the Sandinistas starting in 1981. I was a principal advisor to Misura-

96

Miskito refugees, Honduras. Entire families had to flee FSLN destruction of their communities.

sata-Yatama for the seven rounds of negotiations which were held over a three and a half year period from 1984-1988 in Bogotá, Mexico City and Managua.

While the RN has been fighting to overthrow and replace the Sandinista government, Misurasata-Yatama seeks to remove and replace the invasion-occupation Sandinista regime from the indigenous territories. Though the goals of the two resistance forces are somewhat different, the Sandinistas negotiated using the same tactics and had the same general objectives: 1) stop the armed resistance forces shooting at them, 2) stop U.S. military assistance, 3) fragment civilian support for the resistance and military-political consensus in the resistance, and 4) create favorable international propaganda and support.

At the same time, Sandinistas refused to negotiate the reasons for the two wars against them. Instead, they consistently asserted that they were the legitimate government, that they would not negotiate *any* of their revolution, that the demands of the RN and Yatama were "unconstitutional" and violated the "sovereignty" of the Nicaraguan government, and the only way the conflict can be resolved is when the RN and Yatama accept FSLN amnesty and return home to "integrate" and "reunite the Nicaraguan family." The Sandinistas made no tangible offers to dismantle or reduce their repressive regime, or to democratize, or to release their stranglehold on the Nicaraguan people and Indian nations. What the Sandinistas did do was to use the negotiations as a forum to attack the U.S. for waging war against Nicaragua and to attempt to attack the RN and Yatama negotiation delegations with their FSLN-Ministry of Interior paramilitary goon squads.[1]

Military strength of the resistance forces and U.S. military assistance were far and away the most important influences on the Sandinistas at the negotiation table. Over the three-and a half year period of negotiations between Misurasata-Yatama and the FSLN, the *only* progress (paper only) occurred when the Indian military resistance was winning and the U.S. Congress was about to vote on military assistance. This happened during negotiations in Mexico City on 21 April 1984, the day before a vote in Washington, and in Managua on 2 February 1988, also a day before a military assistance vote in Washington. And in both cases, the paper promises were cheap and useful propaganda for the FSLN because immediately after Congress' rejection of military assistance, the FSLN broke every agreement in the signed accords and not one of the many guarantor governments from Central America or Europe or anywhere else or the media made a squeak of protest.

Sandinista intransigence increased during the periods when Misurasata and Yatama's military punch was reduced due to lack of assistance.

A clear and undeniable pattern emerged from the seven rounds of negotiations: When the Indian resistance had strong military pressure and the threat of more military assistance the FSLN was forced into making some progress in the negotiations, but when the Indian resistance's military capacity was diminished and no military assistance was forthcoming from Washington the FSLN stonewalled and would make no concessions in the negotiations.

Several conclusions can be drawn from the failed negotiations:

1) The resistance lost more than it gained while the FSLN gained more than it lost.

2) At this time, negotiations will not produce democracy or rights because the resistance cannot produce sufficient pressure on the FSLN to make necessary concessions.

3) International pressure is a contradiction in terms. Don't count on it and don't count on it having an effect. Sandinista Nicaragua, like South Africa, is prepared to withstand condemnation from neighbors in the region and from the international community.

✳4) The FSLN reacts to military strength and little else.

5) If negotiations are to be the main means of conflict settlement, then increased military capacity for resistance forces will be the best way to extract concessions from the FSLN.

6) The Frente Sandinista mainly uses negotiations as war by other means to fragment the armed opposition into predictable factions that a) disagree to any negotiations, b) are willing to accept very minimal accords, and c) hold out for real solutions to the war.

7) Sandinista negotiators follow a prepared ideological script in negotiations, but they fare very poorly when they are forced to deviate from the script; they react very slowly and clumsily to new initiatives and usually fall back on knee-jerk assertions of sovereignty and constitutional laws.

8) While, in theory, negotiations may be a means to expose Sandinista intransigence internationally, one should not count on the media to do this. There are four reasons for this: a) many in the media are sympathetic to the FSLN, b) the RN and Yatama resistance forces (and the United States) have very limited media support, c) generally, governments in power get the benefit of the doubt, d) once peace talks begin a false sense of progress is generated and any collapse of the talks is likely be blamed on the insurgency.[2]

9) The Sandinistas have been crystal clear that they will never negotiate the revolution, meaning the basic repressive infrastructure they have imposed on Nicaragua.

10) For the Sandinistas negotiations are a smokeless phase of war but they believe the RN and Yatama negotiate due to weakness and desperation.

Sandinista Comandante Tomás Borge is the Minister of Interior, a member of the FSLN's National Directorate, the only survivor of the FSLN's founders, a leader of the regime's hard-liners, and as head of the FSLN's Autonomy Commission he is commander-in-chief of the occupied Indian and Creole nations, which gives him absolute power over almost one-half of Nicaragua's claimed territory. In May 1988, as head of the FSLN's negotiation delegation, Borge told the Yatama delegation, "When we were fighting in the mountains we *never* considered negotiating with Somoza. We fought to overthrow his government. You call yourselves revolutionaries. Why are you here negotiating?"

The trail of tears

Much of the relationship between the United States and the RN and Yatama has been frustrating. The two armed resistance organizations have been weakened by internal disputes, intermittent and inadequate military assistance, and lack of a clear political agenda that would galvanize Nicaraguans and capture world attention.

The RN is still mired in an image of being a U.S. creation that is only fighting against the Sandinistas but not for a popular and magnetic political and economic program. Thus, both the RN and Washington are dependent on Sandinista oppression to recruit supporters. The RN would be a much more viable organization and alternative if it were to have a dynamic vision and plan for a new Nicaragua based on solid domestic programs that could catapult the country into a good standard of living, good education, good food, and well-paid jobs—a sort of grassroots freedom to work and prosper program.

Without a clear vision and program for a new Nicaragua, anti-Sandinista opposition forces and groups will remain weaker than their potential. Three sectors have considerable potential: the internal opposition, urban uprisings (i.e. Monimbó, Masaya, Subtiava communities, Estelí, Boaco, etc.), and EPS army crossovers. The Sandinistas have forced Nicaraguans to the edge of the water but most people are not going to jump the stream unless they can see what's on the other side and have a half-way rock to help them across.

The RN is not perceived as the good guys. The average person in the United States and Central America sees the RN in only two media contexts: lobbying Washington for money and training recruits in Honduras. And that translates as paid fighters. Anti-Sandinista rhetoric doesn't move people as much as do heroes, a vision for freedom, music, art, poetry, short stories, books, political satire and so on.

Most of this is water over the dam, however. Though the RN combatants are well armed and reasonably well trained, they are faced with being sidelined during 1989 due to the shift from RN military to Central American political pressure on the FSLN to democratize. Threatened with being demobilized in Honduras and Costa Rica, and marginalized from participation in regional agreements concerning Nicaragua, the RN is faced with either sitting this year out—possibly in El Salvador—negotiating with the FSLN from a position of weakness, or trying to run candidates for the municipal and national elections in Nicaragua, promised for February 1990.

The East Coast indigenous nations were the first to fight the Sandinistas and did the most with the least during their now eight-year long resistance. In 1984, at the height of assistance, the Indian and Creole resistance groups had 6,000 fighters, which was less than one-half of the fighting force they could have raised. The resistance has advantages of favorable terrain, sea access, the most anti-Sandinista civilian population anywhere, and strong, positive support for the United States. Many armed fighters are still organized and biding time in Honduras, in small base camps inside the occupied territories, and in cease-fire locations near Puerto Cabezas.

The East Coast occupied territories are vital to the Sandinistas for natural resources and maritime access to Cuba and the Soviet Union. The Sandinistas are the most vulnerable in this region because the majority of the population sees

With husbands fighting or in exile, many Miskito communities in Yapti Tasba have mostly women and children.

them as a brutal occupation army and because the resistance fighters are the best and most effective of any armed group.

At the same time United States and RN relationships with the Indian and Creole leadership of the various organizations have been tumultuous.

Although the longest and in some cases the bitterest conflict, FSLN-Indian war was not mentioned in the 7 August 1987 Esquipulas II accords or in the 14 February 1989 president's summit agreements. Yatama is a political orphan not yet bound to external decisions.

U.S. objectives

U.S. policy objectives

Let us assume that the objectives are three: 1) removal of the Soviets and Cubans from Nicaragua, 2) the end of Sandinista actual or possible support for insurgencies in the region, including Mexico, and 3) the end of the one-party repressive Sandinista state to be replaced by a pluralistic democratic one.

A two-track "shoot and talk" policy has been carried out to achieve these objectives. U.S. military assistance to the RN and to Yatama sought to remove the FSLN from power so that in one stroke all three objectives would be gained. The RN's and Yatama's inability to accomplish this was due as much to external as to internal reasons, such as the Boland Amendment, the Arias Peace Plan, inadequate and intermittent military assistance from the U.S. Congress, as well as internal disputes within the two resistance forces and lack of success projecting a strong political agenda as something to fight for instead of simply fighting against the FSLN. Nevertheless, by the fall of 1987, the RN and Yatama held sway over 70 percent of Nicaragua. Advances were being made to the extent that discussion turned to dealing with the Sandinistas once they were driven from power in Managua, the main thrust of which was to prevent a revolving door of insurgency where the FSLN would go back to the mountains or to the East Coast and start another guerrilla campaign.

The other track was to negotiate with the Sandinistas. "Successful negotiations" (something so theoretical that it should come under SDI funding) was conceived as a foot-in-the-door process whereby the same three objectives might be achieved sequentially over a long period of time as a democratic opposition consolidated and grew in strength. The only problem was that when Yatama and the RN knocked, the Sandinistas didn't open the door. The belief was that faced with an economic death the FSLN would choose political suicide. That is, they would agree to their own destruction. Barring the occurrence of this happening, both the RN and Yatama believed that the negotiations would at least expose the true character of the FSLN. And the FSLN was true to character—recalcitrant and intransigent—but nothing came of it. Getting the FSLN to the negotiation table was easier than getting the international press to write what was happening at the negotiation table.

The shoot-and-talk two-track policy was backed up by an economic blockade strategy that sought to pressure the FSLN on the battlefield and the negotiation table. It was assumed that if the strategy did not do this, at least it would contain the Sandinistas.

At the same time, the U.S. sought political support for these objectives through economic leverage in Costa Rica, Honduras and El Salvador—Nicaragua's neighbors. However, the 1984 election in Costa Rica and the 1987 Arias Peace Plan removed Costa Rica from the Washington plan and added Guatemala and Nicaragua as full partners in a widely touted regional solution.

Still U.S. policy objectives were not obtained by the seven strategies of armed resistance, negotiations, economic blockade, economic assistance to Nicaragua's neighbors and internal opposition, international exposure of FSLN repression, diplomacy, or getting the regional Arias Peace Plan to actually do something. Another potential option is to obtain U.S. objectives by trading with the Soviets—whose support is vital for the FSLN's survival—something of similar value in another world region.

While many of these strategies have produced meaningful results, the upshot is that the FSLN is still in power.

The new United States administration can do several things about this situation:

1) Keep the seven strategies and keep the heat on.

2) Stay off center stage and shift the responsibility for Sandinista Nicaragua to countries in the region, including Venezuela, whose newly elected President Carlos Andrés Pérez has already called on the European community to withhold funding from countries that do not democratize. The 14 February 1989 summit of Central American presidents in El Salvador resuscitated the Esquipulas II peace plan by gaining concessions from Nicaraguan President Daniel Ortega to hold free and open elections by 25 February 1990, allow political parties freedom to campaign and to have equal access to state media, and to release political prisoners. In exchange, the other presidents agreed to demobilize, repatriate or relocate the RN combatants and their families. Although this agreement will not democratize the Sandinistas because elections in themselves will not break the FSLN's institutional stranglehold on the country, it offers the promise that Nicaraguans will take their pent-up grievances to the street, to the ballot box, and to the world. It is also likely that the FSLN will not keep Ortega's promises; the first week after the El Salvador agreement the Sandinistas reneged on freeing contra political prisoners.

3) Pursue a containment policy to further isolate Sandinista Nicaragua. It is already a "bleeding economic ulcer" for the Soviet Union and Cuba, and the outpouring of refugees to neighboring countries and the United States provides a degree

of accountability for external actions that help maintain the Sandinista regime.

4) Concentrate on negotiations—as Mr. Haass suggests—despite the fact that necessary pressure for meaningful FSLN concessions does not exist and declare anything that results to be a U.S. accomplishment.

5) Pursue an agreement with the USSR over Nicaragua (it supplies $400 million a year, 65 percent of Managua's budget) in exchange for an agreement in another world region. On 16 February, on day after the last Soviet soldier left Afghanistan and as the mujahideen close around Kabul and other cities, Soviet leader Mikhail Gorbachev asked President George Bush to help to prevent bloodshed and to support a "representative government."

6) Create other strategies. The United States should develop multiple, flexible and coordinated strategies to achieve policy objectives in Nicaragua and elsewhere in the region. For domestic and international reasons the strategies should project a strong and decisive stance, be perceived as either new or reflecting a new commitment, and they should include Central American reciprocal participation and responsibility. What needs to be changed is the perception of harried, reactive, unsustainable and frustrated strategies. United States policy objectives for Nicaragua and the rest of Central America must be clear and clearly explained to the American people and coordinated with leaders in the region.

Recommendations ⟵ personal

1. _Patience._ Wait a while and let things settle down before going public with any new Central America policy program. Visit Central American countries, invite Central American leaders to Washington, keep the FSLN off balance, project a quiet confidence. As the war closes down it will become perfectly clear regionally and internationally that the FSLN cannot provide the basic needs of Nicaragua. Nicaragua's major

export is refugees, and Central America's problem is the FSLN, not the contras or the war.

2. *Clear public objectives.* Make a clear statement that United States policy towards Sandinista Nicaragua is threefold: a) the removal of Cuban and Soviet military advisors and their massive military buildup; b) the end of Sandinista support to insurgencies in Central America and elsewhere in Latin America, and FSLN provision of a safe haven for international terrorists; and c) the end of repressive, totalitarian rule and the development of a democratic, pluralistic government that represents the diverse interests and aspirations of the Nicaraguan people.

3. *Backstage diplomacy and pressure.* Stay off center stage, encourage Central American and key South American and European leaders to take greater political and economic responsibility in pressuring the FSLN to democratize and demilitarize and to desist from supporting insurgencies elsewhere in the region. The FSLN should have an obligation similar to that being placed on the RN and the United States: demilitarize and end foreign military buildup and advisors.

4. *Levels of engagement.* Concentrate on developing a flexible, sustainable, coordinated policy tied to but not totally dependent upon regional and international involvement. This policy should have at least five levels of engagement: a) provide political support to Nicaraguan opposition groups that are trying to democratize and that will run against the FSLN in the promised 1990 elections (Sandinista law now prohibits the internal opposition from receiving U.S. economic assistance); b) secure Congressional support for economic assistance to the RN and Yatama; c) gear up diplomatic efforts to encourage Central American governments to maintain pressure on the FSLN to demilitarize and to send home the foreign military advisors and to closely monitor Ortega's promises for freedom of political expression; d) rally support for Venezuelan President Carlos Andrés Pérez' call that economic

assistance to Nicaragua be tied to progress in democratization, and e) seek an agreement with the Soviet Union that would restrict Soviet and Cuban assistance to and presence in Nicaragua.

5. *Maintain pressure.* Keep the heat on Sandinista Nicaragua through the economic blockade, diplomatic pressure, regional economic aid, and humanitarian assistance to the RN and Yatama.

6. *Reject negotiations.* It is premature and counterproductive for the U.S. to negotiate with Nicaragua. Acceptance to negotiate would shift the pressure onto the United States. Keep the pressure on Nicaragua to democratize.

7. *The regional peace plan.* The 1987 Esquipulas II plan, the 1988 FSLN-RN Sapoá agreement, and the 1989 El Salvador accord should be supported to the extent that they move Nicaragua closer to democracy and further from oppression. Though no single state in the regional peace process solves the Nicaraguan problem, more detailed and more demanding stages are possible.

8. *Democracy by attrition.* Consider an amnesty program for the Sandinistas to increase erosion of the FSLN. Besides voting the Sandinistas out of office, it is also possible to democratize by attrition. Amnesty and help getting started in a new life in Guatemala, Costa Rica or the United States would be very attractive, it would up the ante on regional responsibility, and would provide a flood of valuable information.

NOTES

1. See my article, "A Close Shave—Sandinista-Style," *Freedom at Issue,* July/August, 1988.
2. State governments are generally reluctant to negotiate with armed insurgencies that seek to overthrow and replace them because the negotiations are believed to give legitimacy to groups that the state characterizes as being illegitimate. The same is true for a state's reluctance to negotiate with distinct nations that are claimed to be nonterritory "ethnic groups" or nonsovereign "autonomous peoples" instead of territorially based peoples who wish to determine their own government (e.g. Kawthoolei, West Papua, East Timor, Palestine, Yapti Tasba, Tigray, Eritrea, Kurdistan, Tamil Eelam, Kanaki, Estonia, Lithuania, Latvia, etc.). However, most negotiations have favored state interests by creating a false international impression that the conflict will be resolved, by creating or increasing fragmentation within the insurgency or resisting nation, and by reducing or ending outside support to the insurgency or resisting nation.

FREEDOM HOUSE BOOKS

General Editor: James Finn

YEARBOOKS

Freedom in the World: Political Rights and Civil Liberties,
Raymond D. Gastil; annuals from 1978-1989.

STUDIES IN FREEDOM

Escape to Freedom: The Story of the International Rescue Committee,
Aaron Levenstein; 1983.
Forty Years: A Third World Soldier at the UN,
Carlos P. Romulo (with Beth Day Romulo); 1986. *(Romulo: A Third World Soldier at the UN,* paperback edition, 1987.)
Today's American: How Free?
edited by James Finn & Leonard R. Sussman, 1986.
Will of the People: Original Democracies in Non-Western Societies,
Raul S. Manglapus; 1987.

PERSPECTIVES ON FREEDOM

Three Years at the East-West Divide,
Max M. Kampelman; (Introductions by Ronald Reagan and Jimmy Carter; edited by Leonard R. Sussman); 1983.
*The Democratic Mask: The Consolidation
of the Sandinista Revolution,*
Douglas W. Payne; 1985.
The Heresy of Words in Cuba: Freedom of Expression & Information,
Carlos Ripoll; 1985.
Human Rights & the New Realism: Strategic Thinking in a New Age,
Michael Novak; 1986.
To License A Journalist?,
Inter-American Court of Human Rights; 1986.
The Catholic Church in China,
L. Ladany; 1987.
Glasnost: How Open? Soviet & Eastern European Dissidents; 1987.
Yugoslavia: The Failure of "Democratic" Communism; 1987.
The Prague Spring: A Mixed Legacy
edited by Jiri Pehe, 1988.
Romania: A Case of "Dynastic" Communism; 1989.

FOCUS ON ISSUES

Big Story: How the American Press and Television Reported and Interpreted the Crisis of Tet-1968 in Vietnam and Washington,
Peter Braestrup; Two volumes 1977;
One volume paperback abridged 1978, 1983.
Afghanistan: The Great Game Revisited,
edited by Rossane Klass; 1988.
Nicaragua's Continuing Struggle: In Search of Democracy,
Arturo J. Cruz; 1988.
La Prensa: The Republic of Paper,
Jaime Chamorro Cardenal; 1988.
The World Council of Churches & Politics, 1975-1986,
J.A. Emerson Vermaat; 1989.
South Africa: Diary of Troubled Times
Nomavenda Mathiane; 1989.
The Unknown War: The Miskito Nation, Nicaragua, and the United States,
Bernard Nietschmann; 1989.

AN OCCASIONAL PAPER

General Editor: R. Bruce McColm

Glasnost and Social & Economic Rights
Valery Chalidze, Richard Schifter; 1988.